ENDORSEM

THE BEST STORY WINS

THE BEST STORY *wins*

How to Leverage
Hollywood Storytelling
in Business and Beyond

Matthew Luhn

NEW YORK

LONDON • NASHVILLE • MELBOURNE • VANCOUVER

THE BEST STORY WINS

How to Leverage Hollywood Storytelling in Business and Beyond

Published in New York, New York, by Morgan James Publishing. Morgan James is a trademark of Morgan James, LLC. www.MorganJamesPublishing.com

The Morgan James Speakers Group can bring authors to your live event. For more information or to book an event visit The Morgan James Speakers Group at www.TheMorganJamesSpeakersGroup.com.

Pixar is a registered trademark of the Disney Company.

ISBN 9781642790207 paperback
ISBN 9781642790658 case laminate
ISBN 9781642790214 eBook
Library of Congress Control Number: 2018937000

Cover Design by:
Matthew Luhn

Interior Design by:
Chris Treccani
www.3dogcreative.net

Edited by:
David Drury

In an effort to support local communities, raise awareness and funds, Morgan James Publishing donates a percentage of all book sales for the life of each book to Habitat for Humanity Peninsula and Greater Williamsburg.

Get involved today! Visit
www.MorganJamesBuilds.com

To my Dad

– TABLE OF CONTENTS –

- INTRODUCTION -

The most powerful person in the world is the storyteller. The storyteller sets the vision, values, and agenda of an entire generation that is to come.

–STEVE JOBS

For over twenty-five years my job title has been Guy Who Makes People Cry. Yes, I'm in the business of making kids and grown adults cry in theaters, living rooms, airplanes, and anywhere else they can view a movie. But along with making people cry, I'm also in the business of making people laugh, cheer, think, and most importantly, experience something that transforms their life.

What is my job? I'm a storyteller. From developing stories and characters at Pixar Animation Studios for over twenty years, to writing on films and TV shows in Hollywood, to training business leaders and marketing professionals how to craft stories that strengthen their brand, I love to create stories and to teach others how to become better storytellers. How did this become my job? Well, it all started in a toy store, because when I was born my mom and dad owned and operated more independent toy stores in the San Francisco Bay Area than anyone in the toy business.

Our family-run operation was called Jeffrey's Toys. Not a bad way to grow up, right? Imagine waking up on your birthday and your parents saying, "Pick out a toy, any toy." The only downside was figuring out who my *real* friends were, as opposed to the ones coming over just to play with my complete collection of *Star Wars* toys.

But my mom and dad didn't start the family toy stores. My grandparents owned and operated the toy stores before them, and my great-grandparents owned and operated the toy stores before my grandparents, and my great-great-grandfather Charlie had nothing to do with the toy stores. He actually hated toys and kids, and ran illegal gambling out of his cigar shop in San Francisco.

Other than Charlie, everyone else in my family has had something to do with the toy stores in one way or another. Why? Because my family has always believed in creating a place where children and adults feel inspired to play, imagine, and have fun, one toy at a time. This is what my family has been doing for as long as I can remember—they love creating an experience for people when they enter a Jeffrey's Toys store. And what is the best way to inspire people to feel something, in entertainment or business?—through great storytelling that will lead them to action and change. The person, company, or fictional character that tells the best story will always make the strongest connection with the audience. Wouldn't you like to be that person?

All people crave stories. We love to hear them, see them, tell them, and retell them. We express our desires and our fears through storytelling. This telling is what gives us life and gives our lives meaning. When you and I post a Tweet, we're telling a story. When we share an image on Instagram or Snapchat, we're telling a story. Even the most mundane things we do are full of movement and emotion that make people feel something: a handshake, a wave, a home-cooked meal, a furrowed brow, or a middle finger. They all tell a story. Everything you or I do is wrapped up in story, from a novel, to a film, to a sales pitch, to an image affiliated with your brand, to a family-run toy store.

The funny thing is, my dad never really wanted to own or operate the family-run toy store. Although he loved toys, he had a different dream, one he had had since he was a kid. He wanted to become an animator and work for Walt Disney. All through elementary, junior, and high school my dad spent more time drawing cartoon characters in the corners of his schoolbooks than he did reading them. He even carried his dream of becoming an animator with him through the Vietnam War, filling dozens of sketchbooks while serving overseas in the army. When he returned home, he announced to his dad—my grandfather, a World War II Marine veteran—that he didn't want to work in the toy stores. He wanted to be a Disney animator instead.

"Son, there ain't no way you're going to become an animator," my grandfather replied. "You can't make a living as an artist. Plus, I need you to help me run the toy stores." So, the Marine logic won the battle of wills, and my dad's dream of becoming a Disney animator was set aside. He later got married, had a son (me), and, sure enough, worked day in and day out at the toy stores.

Then one day when I was about four years old, my dad stayed home from the toy store with a terrible stomachache. Wanting to cheer him up, I did the only thing I could do as a four-year-old; I drew him a picture. The picture was a sketch of my dad with a stomachache. I thought it was a pretty good likeness, right down to his stomach filled with all kinds of swirls and squiggly lines to represent the kind of pain I imagined he felt. When my dad saw the drawing, he pointed at me and said, "You. You are the chosen one. You will live my dream. You will be that Disney animator." These may not have been his *exact* words, but that was the takeaway from my childhood.

From that point on I became my dad's young apprentice. He sat and drew with me all the time. We drew on placemats at restaurants, on the wooden fences that surrounded our backyard, even on the beams of the Eiffel Tower (I sincerely apologize, Paris. I was only ten years old and my dad said it was OK). He bought me how-to-draw books and art supplies, and even transformed a cardboard refrigerator box into a small movie booth—complete with a working black-and-white TV, tiny chair, and bedsheet curtain—so I could watch cartoons. While most parents were reading their kids bedtime stories like *The Very Hungry Caterpillar* and *Winnie-the-Pooh*, my dad was reading me *Tales of the Crypt* comic books and issues of *Mad* magazine before I would gently fall asleep. But it didn't stop there. Once a week, after being dropped off by my mom in the morning at elementary school, I would then be picked up about thirty minutes later by my dad. He would tell the school secretary that I had a doctor or dentist appointment that day, but the real reason he was pulling me out of school was because we were going to the movies. This is no joke. He figured that we could avoid the long lines that accompany a new release by seeing that movie in the middle of the day, while most kids were still at school. I had the best dad any kid could wish for.

At first all of the movies we went to see were animated, like *The Jungle Book*, *Robin Hood*, and *The Secret of NIMH*. Then after we saw all the animated films, he started taking me to live-action movies like *Star Wars*, *Young Frankenstein*, and *Kingdom of the Spiders*. He

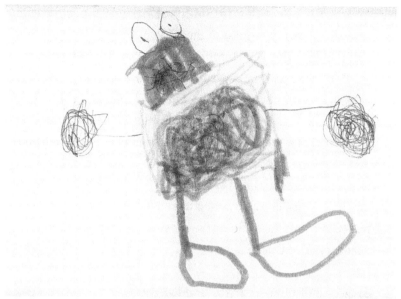

had a particular fascination for sci-fi and horror. Of course, taking your kid to go see *Poltergeist* at the wide-eyed age of nine is not a great idea. I had nightmares for months! Even so, my father's passion for art, animation, and movies rubbed off on me, and by the time I was in high school, I began making films and animating with an old Super 8 camera. It seemed natural to learn the animation process and strive to make, in a very primitive way, the magic my dad had shared with me.

While in high school, I also discovered a college that specialized in animation. I desperately wanted to attend. The college was called CalArts (California Institute of the Arts), designed and founded by the legendary Walt Disney himself. This was *the* place to learn about animation.

By no small miracle, I was granted entrance, and off I went. I loved every minute of my training. The room number of the CalArts animation department was and still is A113. If you're a Pixar or Disney enthusiast (aka animation nerd) like I am, you probably know "A113" shows up in every Pixar film. From Mater's license plate in the film *Cars* to Mike and Sully's dorm room number in *Monsters University* to dozens of other hidden places in Pixar films. Why? Because almost all of the directors, storyboard artists, writers, character designers, and animators from Pixar attended CalArts. Alums also include the creators of animated TV shows like *The Powerpuff Girls, Dexter's Laboratory, We Bare Bears*, and directors and actors like Tim Burton, Pee-Wee Herman, and David Hasselhoff. I even heard that the Hoff and Pee-Wee were roommates! Now *that* would make a great TV show.

During my first year at CalArts, I made an animated film called *Steward Skyler Saves the Day*. To my surprise, it caught the attention of a director working on the brand-new, prime-time, animated hit *The Simpsons*. I was asked to come into the studio and take a *Simpsons* animation test. Yes, there really was and still is a *Simpsons* animation test that confirms whether or not you can draw Bart, Homer, Marge, Lisa, and Maggie. I passed the test and was offered a job as an animator on *The Simpsons*, but declined, letting them know I had to finish my degree first . . . actually no . . . I immediately left school and began animating on the third season of *The Simpsons*, as the youngest animator at nineteen years old. At this point, I had in a way accomplished my dad's goal—*ahem*—my goal of becoming an animator. But something was about to change.

One day, while animating on the episode "Homer Alone," I stumbled into the story room at *The Simpsons*. Now I had always imagined writers on a TV show to be moody individuals, sitting alone in a dark office behind a keyboard churning out script pages, but instead I witnessed an eclectic group made up of comic book artists, Harvard grads, and comedians, who all had one thing in common— they were great storytellers. Even Conan O'Brien spent time as a writer on *The Simpsons*. As I witnessed their brainstorming process for turning out scripts, I instantly knew that *this* was what I wanted to do. I wanted to do more than animate stories other people had written, I wanted to create those stories. While my dad's passion was animation, I realized that the part of the animation process I loved the most was the big picture, the story itself, the invention of characters and the adventures they would go on.

But I had no idea how I could make the transition from animator to storyteller. I also didn't want to let down my dad and not meet the expectations he, and my whole family, had for me. But deep down inside, I really wanted to be part of that magical story process.

After finishing up on the third season of *The Simpsons*, I decided two things. First, as a San Francisco Bay Area native I didn't want to live in Los Angeles for the rest of my life. Second, I would do anything to become a storyteller.

Then one day, out of the blue, I was offered a job to work at a small startup animation studio in the Bay Area. Although it was risky taking an animation job at a place that had no experience making animated films—only animated commercials and advertising shorts for computer products—and moving far from Los Angeles, where all the "real" animation jobs were, I took a chance.

The studio at the time was only made up of eighty people, with the dream of making the very first computer-generated (CG) animation film. They called themselves Pixar.

This was no traditional animation studio. Director John Lasseter and the other writers wanted to make an animated film that did *not* take place in a fairy-tale village and had *no* prince or princess singing the standard "I Want" song. Not to mention the film was going to be entirely animated in a computer. Not a single cel of hand-drawn animation would be used. It promised to be something totally different. The studio was also owned by a newbie to the film industry, Steve Jobs, who was suffering from a streak of bad luck after being let go from his own company, Apple, and then creating a failed computer called NeXT.

When I started at Pixar in 1992, I was hired as one of the first twelve computer animators to work on their first animated film, *Toy Story*. Almost everyone in the animation industry believed that this film was going to flop.

My very first assignment on *Toy Story* was to animate the little toy green army men coming to life—without losing the plastic bases they were attached to. To get the animation correct, I actually screwed my shoes to a wooden rectangular board and filmed myself walking, running, crawling, and even leaping off of office desks all over the Pixar studio. I was determined to make that animation as accurate as possible.

But once again, the part of the production that was most interesting to me was the story. This is what I really wanted to be doing. I wanted to help create the characters, draw the storyboards, and stitch the stories together. So, every day after I finished my animation, I would wander into the story room and ask if anyone on the story team needed any help cleaning up storyboards, filling in color, or anything else. Pretty soon I spent all of my evenings and weekends helping out the story team after my animation was done. The possibility of moving into the story department was in sight.

Then one day, the Disney Company (who was funding *Toy Story*) decided to pull the plug on the film. Their reason? They said that the main character Woody was unappealing. We were devastated, but John Lasseter, *Toy Story*'s director, was *really* devastated. As John met with each one of us one by one, he apologized for letting us down and promised to call us back if the Disney Company ever changed their minds.

My friends in Los Angeles lined up to say, "I told you so," as I was now stuck in Northern California with no work. Strangely enough, I saw this as an opportunity. I suddenly had all the time in the world to learn more about storytelling! Making some phone calls, I got in touch with a small commercial animation company in San Francisco and began storyboarding and writing for fast-food commercials, breakfast cereal commercials, and animated TV shows. It was a great way to get my feet wet in the world of storytelling. And of course, I also worked in the family toy stores to help pay my bills.

One year later, Pete Docter, the head of animation at Pixar, called me up and offered me my old job back. He said that the Pixar story team had managed to fix the character problems in *Toy Story* and had the green light from Disney to move forward. I was torn. While grateful for the call, what I really wanted was to work in the Pixar story department. I declined the job offer, sharing with Pete my passion for storytelling. Pete could tell I was determined and said he would keep me in mind if anything popped up.

Months went by as I continued to work at the small commercial animation studio in San Francisco. Eventually, that work dried up. I hopped around from one job to the next, feeling as if I had made the worst decision of my life by turning down the animation job at Pixar. I was living back at my mom and dad's house and even forced to borrow money from a friend to pay my car insurance. Then, out of the blue, Pixar called. They were going to make *Toy Story 2* and needed an extra member on their story team. Hallelujah! I joined the team and never looked back. I had no idea then, but this was the beginning of a twenty-year story career at Pixar, working on ten films, five animated shorts, and two TV specials. And through it all, we were having fun, just like when I was in high school creating films with my friends.

Then one day, while perusing *Wired* magazine, I came upon an article stating that Pixar had created more globally loved and financially successful movies in a row than any other film studio in the history of film. Yes, we had created more movie hits in a row than Warner Brothers, Universal Studios, Paramount, and MGM. How did this happen? It was more than just great computer animation or character designs or color or music. It was because of great storytelling. Story is king at Pixar. Throughout the years—while working as a story guy on *Toy Story 2, Toy Story 3, Monsters Inc., Finding Nemo, UP, Cars, Ratatouille, Monsters University,* and as a writer and story consultant at other companies—I've come to realize that great stories not only make for great novels, plays, movies, and television, but also for successful businesses and brands. Whether your audience is sitting in theater seats or walking down toy store aisles or buying something online, engaging them or making a sale comes down to telling a story that really stirs people to feel something.

While I still lead a life of writing scripts and coming up with story ideas, I also love to share the principles of great storytelling with people working in the worlds of sales, marketing, and speaking, helping them strengthen their brand, make authentic connections, and drive their audience to action through an inspiring story.

Why are stories so meaningful? Resonating so effectively with everyone, regardless of age, gender, and culture? It's because great stories, when told well, are memorable, impactful, and personal. Oxford's dictionary defines a story as: "an account of imaginary or real people and events told for entertainment. An account of past events in someone's life or in the development of something." Old or new, strictly true or wildly made-up, great stories move people. We are drawn to all kinds, whether it is "You won't believe what happened to me this weekend!" or "A priest, a rabbi, and a duck walk into a bar." We are drawn like magnets to great stories. They intrigue us. They put voice to the things we want and believe in.

When you share statistics, data, or information with people without a story, they only retain about 5 percent of the information if you ask them about it ten minutes later. That's pretty depressing, right? Especially if your job is running numbers all day long or collecting and distributing data for a living. Yes, big data is changing everything, but without a great story to create an emotional pull, the information will be forgotten by your customers, clients, or fellow employees at your next board meeting. Here's the thing, when you deliver that same information to people with a story or event woven around it, people remember it. They actually retain more of the information. According to Jerome Bruner, a cognitive psychologist, facts are 22 times more likely to be remembered if they are part of a story. It even works with the driest of facts. Adding a story may seem like a subtle move, but it begins to change everything.

When I was in elementary school, I was the kid drawing in his textbooks and looking out the window. When teachers shared information with the class that consisted heavily of facts, numbers, names, and dates, I could be counted on to forget it all almost immediately. I now understand why. There was no story or event wrapped around the information. Rudyard Kipling, author of *Tarzan* and *The Jungle Book* said, "If history were taught in the form of stories, it would never be forgotten."

Consider how the jewelry retailer Tiffany & Company combines narrative, colors, typeface, and visuals to tell a memorable story. Their trademark robin-egg Tiffany blue creates the feeling of tranquility and escape, their typeface and logo feel elegant and sophisticated, and the photographs and images used in their stores, websites, and ads communicate love and romance. All together, they tell a memorable brand story that you know well—even if you have never shopped there. What people will retain instantly jumps from 5 percent to 65 percent when the content is embedded in a story. Not only do they retain it, they feel more connected to it.

In the Pixar movie *Inside Out*, audiences were not only treated to an entertaining story but also educated on how and why some memories go to the memory dump, while others stick around. Without fail, memories stick around inside your head when they are wrapped in a story or an event.

There is a scientific reason why stories stick in our minds. Way back in our evolution, when humans developed the ability to speak, we communicated about life or death situations, like being chased by a tiger, successfully hunting a bison, or avoiding poisonous plants. We know that storytelling was important to our early ancestors because we have "storyboards" of those life lessons that date back thousands of years painted on cave walls. The ancient people that learned the lessons of those stories lived, and the ones that didn't died.

Along with being memorable, stories are impactful. Stories take us on a roller-coaster ride, a journey through high moments (happiness, anticipation, surprise) and low moments (sadness, fear, anger) that actually affect our bodies on a chemical level. Science has revealed that the chemicals in our tears produced by laughter are different than the chemicals in our tears produced by sadness. When we see or hear people—or even animated toys, robots, or rats—laughing, smiling, or sharing stories of suspense, dopamine and endorphins are released in our bodies; when we see or hear anything sad or somber, oxytocin is released. When we place these sad and happy moments next to each other in a story, we build an amusement park ride for people's hearts and minds. Ups and downs, tension and release, you've created a story that keeps an audience sitting on the edge of their seats.

The opening of the movie *UP* has become famous for making people laugh, cry, and feel something. In that first sequence we see a young man and woman fall in love, get married, build a house, work together, and dream about having children. These kinds of happy and funny moments filled with anticipation and suspense release a heavy dose of dopamine and endorphins throughout our bodies. Then we see the couple at the hospital discovering that the woman cannot have a child. Suddenly, our happy chemicals come crashing down like a ton of bricks, as oxytocin courses through our bodies. We can't help but become teary-eyed and choked-up, feeling empathetic for the characters. Then we see the man cheer up his wife by giving her an adventure journal, and together they plan to travel one day to South America to visit Paradise Falls. Our happy chemicals surge again, making us smile. But then we see that the couple can never save up enough money to go on their adventure, and our happy chemicals crash again. The years go by, and they both grow older. Then one day the old man remembers the promise to his wife and sells his pocket watch to get enough money to buy those two plane tickets to Paradise Falls. We are feeling good again. Actually, we're feeling great! They're finally going to go on that trip together! But before the old man can give his wife the tickets she collapses, is taken to the hospital, and passes away. What?! Yes, and at this point, no matter how bad someone needs to use the restroom or wants to get something to eat, they're not going to leave their seat because they want to know what's going to happen to that old man. Wouldn't you love to deliver a sales pitch to a client or share your company's vision internally and have that same can't-leave-your-seat effect on your audience?

Great leaders and speakers use this technique of tension and release all the time. They know how to take an audience on a ride from the ordinary world, up to what things could be, back to the ordinary world, leading to an epic ending that seals the deal.

One of the great things about working at Pixar for over half my life was the chance to spend time with Steve Jobs, who was a great storyteller. When he delivered information or shared his vision for Pixar, he would always tie it into a story.

When Jobs debuted the iPhone in 2007 at the Macworld Expo in San Francisco, he used this up-and-down kind of storytelling. He began his presentation by saying, "This is a day I've been looking forward to for two-and-a-half years." His excitement spread throughout the crowd. "Today Apple is going to reinvent the phone with a new device called the iPhone." The audience was transfixed and happy chemicals were running high, but then he paused and took everyone down by saying that every smartphone that has ever been created wasn't smart, but stupid. While the audience's sad chemicals were still being released, Jobs quickly changed the direction and announced, "But my smartphone is as smart as a computer," and everyone jumped out of their seats. Then he took everyone down again, "Haven't you noticed that every smartphone is clunky to use with a stylus pen?" And then he took everyone back up, "But my phone is completely touchscreen. With a swipe of your finger you can navigate all the functions on the iPhone." At this point the audience nearly exploded from the excitement. If you want to tell a story that is memorable—and moves people to act—you must take your audience on a roller-coaster ride of emotions.

All the decisions we make in life—from what shoes we wear, to who we date, to what shows we watch—are made based on who or what has made us feel something. Big or small, our decisions are made on the right side of our brain, which is triggered by our emotions. Yes, later on we'll rationalize these decisions with the left side of our brain, deciding if we made a good choice or not, so it's important that the product, solution, or idea has substance as well. And when a story is memorable and impactful, whoever is telling the story, whether the author of a novel, the actor on a screen, or the CEO of a company, a personal connection is made with that storyteller. Whether it is Tom Hanks in *Forest Gump* sharing stories that changed the lives of strangers sitting next to him at a bus stop, or Steve Jobs sharing stories about Apple to inspire his employees, storytelling has the power to create a personal connection with a single person or an entire company. Incorporating story into your personal or professional life is the best way to inspire people to make decisions.

My hope in this book is to share with you the simple steps to becoming a better storyteller, unleashing the power of story in your presentations, marketing strategies, global branding, sales techniques, and leadership.

- We crave stories because they give voice to the things we want and believe in. We express our desires and our fears through storytelling. What are some of your favorite novels, movies, or TV shows?
- The memories we retain are the ones connected to a compelling story or event. Can you recall some of your most memorable personal or professional moments?
- Share stories that are funny, happy, or suspenseful to create high levels of dopamine or endorphins, and sad or somber stories to create high levels of oxytocin. Include both happy and sad moments in your story or pitch to keep your audience on the edge of their seats.
- Great stories are not just for entertainment, but also for creating successful businesses and brands. Can you name

three of your favorite businesses or brands? Do they have a memorable, impactful, and personal story? What stories are the beating heart under the surface of your company or brand?

- CHAPTER 1 -

The Hook

An opening line should invite the reader to begin the story. It should say: Listen. Come in here. You want to know about this.

—STEVEN KING

No one expects a leisurely stroll down a city street to turn into an encounter with a giant hairy gorilla—but that's exactly what my grandfather had in mind when he placed "Joe" in the front window of our family's toy store. Joe was a six-foot-tall stuffed toy gorilla, complete with a name tag stuck to his matted chest that read "Joe." Not only was the gorilla massive, he was mechanical, with a body that turned and waved to everyone passing by. The idea for the gorilla came about when my grandfather, fed up with people walking right past his toy store day in and day out without venturing in, decided something needed to be done to catch their attention. So he bought a stuffed gorilla and put him to work.

Needless to say, "Joe" got people's attention. They would turn and look every time. They would stop in their tracks, they would yelp, they would jump back, startled. They often laughed out loud or grabbed the person next to them. But most importantly, Joe brought people into the store. The passersby wanted to know more. What was going on inside that store? They needed to find out. It was a great hook. A hook that got people talking. A hook that invited people to walk into the toy store and buy a toy before they left.

My grandfather didn't want to gain customers by accident or by force, but by invitation. He wanted to arouse curiosity. Other hooks he created included launching water rockets that landed in the middle of foot traffic and having his employees—himself too—dress up in giant toy animal costumes while working at the store. He even displayed my father in the front window of the toy store with a bottle of glue, paints, and new model kits so that people walking by would stop to watch the kid in the window happily building a model airplane or model car, and want to enter the store.

Research tells us that the attention span of the average person is eight seconds. You have eight seconds to convince people that you've got something worth hearing about before they zone out, tune out, or check out. Be it a pitch to investors, a company presentation, or an advertisement, if you can't catch the attention of your audience within eight seconds, you've already lost. So, how do you grab an audience's attention within eight seconds? With a great hook. Like a gorilla in a window.

Now, more than ever, our attention is at a premium. We are busy, easily distracted, short on time, our noses buried in our cell phones. Before you can get someone to go into your store, check out your website, or learn about your great product or idea, you have to convince them that you have a story worth listening to.

You Only Get One Chance to Make a First Impression

I know what it's like when you're casting about for a great hook. I have pitched to Hollywood directors and Fortune 500 CEOs with very short attention spans. So what goes into creating a great hook? You need to catch people with something unusual, unexpected, action-driven, or that raises a clear conflict.

When creating eight-second hooks, it helps to start with a question like a "what if" scenario. For example, "What if superheroes were banned from saving people?" That was the hook for *The Incredibles*, which took the "ordinary" world of superheroes saving people and turned it into an unusual situation. Your audience is now hooked and asking, "Why and how did they get banned?"

Or, "What if a rat wanted to become a French chef?" This hook from *Ratatouille* is unexpected, because why in the world would a rat want to cook?

Or, "What if the asteroid that destroyed the dinosaurs had missed?" The image of the asteroid about to crash into our planet from the movie *The Good Dinosaur* makes for a great action-driven hook.

Or, "What if a child's favorite toy is replaced by a newer toy?" This hook from the movie *Toy Story* raises a clear conflict.

Hooks that set up an intriguing question work like magic. This is true not just for film, but also for inspiring your employees or motivating customers to buy your product or service.

For example, when Steve Jobs introduced the iPod in 2001 his hook was: "What if you could put a thousand songs in your pocket?" This was unheard of. At the time, the only way you could listen to music on the go was with an eight-to-twelve-song cassette tape stuffed in a Walkman. Steve shared something unusual in eight seconds that grabbed his audience's attention.

Or, how about Elon Musk's hook for Tesla: "What if a company created an electric car that was aesthetically appealing?"

Whether for *The Incredibles,* Apple, or Tesla, good "what if" hooks disrupt our ordinary world and catch our attention. This hook can be positive or negative. It depends on the story you want to tell. In the case of Tesla, the hook is positive, offering up a solution to an ordinary world where cool-looking cars only run on fossil fuels. For *The Incredibles*, the hook is a negative, setting up how an ordinary world of superheroes would be turned upside down if superheroes were banned from saving people.

To get your hook across in eight seconds you must be as clear and concise as possible. Don't focus on how many words it will take you to convince people, but how few. Albert Einstein said it best: "If you can't explain it simply, you don't understand it well enough." Here are a couple of great opening lines to movies that have clear and concise hooks:

- *Goodfellas*: "As far back as I can remember, I always wanted to be a gangster."
- *Toy Story*: "Alright, everyone, this is a stickup! Don't anybody move!"
- *Ferris Bueller's Day Off*: "The key to faking out the parents is the clammy hands. It's a good nonspecific symptom; I'm a big believer in it."

In Arianna Huffington's book *Thrive* she jolted her audience with the first sentence: "On the morning of April 6, 2007, I was lying on the floor of my home office in a pool of blood." What a hook!

Hooks can be visual, too. Like movie posters, single images in a magazine, or a gorilla in a window. For example, a woman who works at a health insurance company told me how she uses her dented laptop to sell insurance. How does she do that? Well, right before she starts her sales pitch with a customer she opens up her dented laptop. The customer can't help but ask what happened to her computer. This curiosity sets up the beginning of a story. The agent shares how one day someone pulled out in front of her, and she was forced to slam on the brakes. Two things happened. She suffered minor whiplash, and her laptop, which she had left on the dashboard, was thrown around the car and damaged. Due to her injury, she went to the hospital—and experienced firsthand how the very health company she worked for actually operated. She was overwhelmed by the great service she received—everyone treated her well, even though they had no idea she worked for the company. The experience made her truly proud of her company.

You may not have a dented laptop, but you probably have something lying around that begs a story. Can you think of visual hooks you could use at your next important pitch? Do you have something that is memorable or meaningful to you, which might serve as a great lead-in to a story that relates to your product or vision for your company?

Don't forget the other senses to hook an audience: smell, sound, touch, and taste. Free food, candy, perfume, hand lotion, or wine are all great ways to catch your audience's attention, which could then lead to conversations and customer action. Sometimes customers simply like the music playing outside a store and wander in. At our family toy store, we play familiar music from kid's movies, hand out freshly made popcorn that smells and tastes great, have toys set up for people to play with (like wooden trains and windup toys), and display lots of toy-related posters and art on our walls along with the history of Jeffrey's Toys. The key words are *simple* and *effective*.

Loglines and the Elevator Pitch

A hook is not a story. It's just a taste of what your story could be. In order to transform your hook into a story, you will need to create a *logline,* which contains the four elements that have been used in storytelling for thousands of years:

1. A hero
2. A goal
3. One or more obstacles (sometimes this involves a villain)
4. A transformation

A logline can be told in three minutes, in thirty seconds, or even in a single sentence. In the entertainment industry, people sometimes call the logline an *elevator pitch*. If you found yourself in the elevator with a big-time movie director and only had a few minutes to pitch your amazing idea, what would you say? In business, the logline would be the mission statement.

For example, the logline for *Monsters Inc.* was "When Sully, the best 'scarer' in the Monster World, accidentally befriends a human child and discovers that children are not toxic, he risks getting fired from his job, being thrown in jail, and losing his best friend in order to expose the truth that scaring human kids is wrong." Yes, it's a mouthful, but this single sentence imparts the entire movie in a clear and concise way.

1. Who is the hero? Sully, a monster that scares kids.
2. What is his goal? To save a child while exposing the truth that scaring kids is wrong.
3. What are the obstacles? Being fired, losing his best friend, and getting banished.
4. What is the transformation? Sully will move from naïveté to awareness.

Facebook's logline/mission statement: "give people the power to build community and bring the world closer together, to stay connected with friends and family, to discover what's going on in the world, and to share and express what matters to them."

1. Who is the hero? All people.
2. What is Facebook's goal? To help people build community and bring the world closer together.
3. What are the obstacles? The world is a big place and it's difficult to stay connected.
4. What is the transformation? People will be able to connect with friends and family, discover what's going on in the world, and share and express what matters to them.

Whether the hero is a single person or a company, they need to go on a journey to reach their goal. The goal might be to defeat a dragon, reach new customers, or build a better product. The hero must also face obstacles in order to create tension and uncertainty in the audience, keeping people engaged until the very end. These obstacles can be roadblocks, reversals, or twists, like a killer clown, a scheming competitor, or a spaceship that fails to jump to light speed.

By the end of the story, the hero or heroes have changed, and if done well, have engendered a change in the audience as well.

Give it a try. Write down the name of a person or group you're currently working with or want to work with. What is their goal? What obstacles are keeping them from their goal? How could your products, services, or solutions help them reach their goal and experience a positive change?

Below are four examples of different loglines:

- What if there was a way to organize a company's data to help them better reach and influence their current and potential customers?
- What if low-income families were offered free financial services and programs to help them achieve home ownership and economic stability?
- What if there was a toy store that could transport you back to a simpler time when having fun and playing was the most important thing in life?
- What if a product could turn everyday garbage into clean-burning fuel for any DeLorean?

Yes, that last logline is for the "Mr. Fusion" product from the end of *Back to the Future*, but you get the idea.

Now that you know what goes into a great logline and hook, our next step in chapter 2 is how to keep your audience's attention through transformational stories of characters changing.

- You have about eight seconds to hook the attention of any audience.
- A great hook is something unusual, unexpected, action-driven, or raises a clear conflict.
- You must know your idea well enough to explain it in as few words as possible.
- Pitching your hook as a question, like a "what if," is a great way to engage with your audience.
- Use a hero, goal, set of obstacles, and a transformation when creating a logline.
- Use visual hooks to grab an audience's attention.

- **CHAPTER 2** -

Character Transformation

Somewhere inside all of us is the power

to change the world.

–Roald Dahl

When Disneyland opened on July 17, 1955, a promise of change was inscribed on a golden plaque displayed above the main archway leading guests into the Happiest Place on Earth: "Here you leave today and enter the world of yesterday, tomorrow, and fantasy." A personal promise from Walt Disney to his guests, that what they were about to experience, through the attractions, environment, and employees, was going to change them in a positive way.

While a great hook catches our attention, it is the promise of change that brings us to the edge of our seats and keeps us listening. Because the very next thing an audience wants to know after you hook them is *how* are you going to change them. Are you going to make them healthier? Wealthier? Happier? Inspired?

We are attracted to the possibilities of personal transformation. When we see people adopting a new idea or way of thinking it piques our interest, and we want to know how they did it and why. But while change is exciting, it also scares us. Change pulls us out of our comfort zones. Change requires courage, dedication, and effort.

Whether you're making a pitch to a prospective customer or motivating your employees, it's important to lead them through a transformation to inspire change. They may be quite resistant to change at the onset, but that resistance will melt away if you offer them an exciting path to that change.

It took Walt Disney a whole lot of ingenuity, dedication, and effort to change the world's perception of carnivals and amusement parks when he first pitched the idea for Disneyland. Most people thought Disneyland was going to bomb. Hollywood and the press dubbed Walt's park idea, "Walt's folly." Walt Disney's brother Roy believed the project would lead them to financial ruin. Even the banks wouldn't loan Walt the money to build the first Disneyland. He had no choice but to borrow money against his life insurance and even mortgaged his own house to raise the funds. The bankers, investors, press, and others were skeptical because it was something new and different.

One of the ways Walt was able to change the minds of his skeptics and get them excited about Disneyland was through his TV show, *The Wonderful World of Disney.* Every Sunday night, Walt would highlight stories representing life in one of Disneyland's themed lands: Adventureland, Tomorrowland, Fantasyland, and Frontierland. For example, Davy Crockett and other heroes of the Old West were featured to get people excited about Frontierland, an animated cartoon like *Alice in Wonderland* would be shown for Fantasyland, *20,000 Leagues under the Sea* for Adventureland, and a short about outer space for Tomorrowland. Along with these stories, Walt would also share conceptual artwork for his vision of Disneyland. These stories and visuals worked their magic, and people couldn't wait to go to Disneyland!

Less than 15 percent of the population is open to trying new things without any outside motivation or a traumatic event forcing them to change. The rest of us don't like to change, even when we know it is good for us. This is why most people prefer the path of least resistance when faced with change. We pick the low-hanging fruit, instead of working harder to get the juicier fruit farther out of reach. We don't wake up in the morning and say, "Today, I'm going to stop smoking" or "Today, I'm going to start spending more time with my kids." Instead, we put off change until something traumatic happens, like a heart attack or when our kids grow up and move away.

So how can you get people to change?

By telling them a story.

Storytelling is the most effective way to change minds, behaviors, and philosophies. Why? Because people look to the actions of others to determine their own. When fictional or nonfictional characters go through a believable transformation, the audience is changed as well. This process is called neural coupling. Neural coupling is when the brain activity of the storyteller and the person listening mirror each other; the listener is affected by the storyteller's journey and the characters who are changing within the story.

These stories can take the form of myths, legends, fairy tales, cautionary tales, films, television shows, song lyrics, or casual conversations around the watercooler. But they all have one thing in common: they teach a lesson that changes the way we think and feel. Employing a character or characters that go through a change is the best way to inspire a change in your audience.

A few years back, after giving a keynote presentation on storytelling at a financial institution, a soft-spoken man came up to me with tears in his eyes. He told me how he and his wife had struggled for years to have a baby. Mentally and physically exhausted, they began to lose hope, and one night got in an argument that almost led to them getting separated. Before things got out of hand, they put their argument on hold and went to a movie. The movie was *UP*. During the first twelve minutes of the movie they were in tears as they watched the main characters, a young married couple in love, also struggling and failing to have a baby. But in the movie, the married couple didn't give up on each other. Instead they turned their inability to have a baby into a different passion—planning an epic trip to South America. By the end of the movie, the soft-spoken guy and his wife chose to stay together, stopped trying to have a baby, and found other passions to build their life around. Then, years later, when they least expected it, they had a baby. In the following years, they had two more. The man wanted to thank me for my role in making the movie.

When stories are done right, they can generate a powerful dose of empathy. What exactly is empathy? Empathy occurs the moment we imagine ourselves in someone else's shoes, adopting their point of view, which creates a personal connection.

When you share success stories about yourself (or about other people) struggling to obtain something, your audience roots for you to reach your goal. This in turn inspires them to pursue goals that may seem too difficult in their lives. Your transformational experience— your success story—can inspire others to change and take action, like trying something new at their company, improving the way they communicate with their customers, or becoming a more confident leader. The deeper you take your listener into another character's life experiences and heart, the more powerful and transformative your stories can be.

My grandfather believed in the power of transformation and created positive experiences in his toy stores that were capable of changing people. He knew that once he lured people into his store, he had to give them a good reason to stay. To help them overcome their fear of change, he created places in the store where kids and adults could test out toys and have fun. My grandfather even built a giant slot-car racetrack on the bottom level in one toy store that could only be accessed by zipping down a colorful helter-skelter slide. At Jeffrey's Toys, customers were invited to be transformed and take those positive experiences home with them. Like Walt Disney said, "Do what you do so well that they will want to see it again and bring their friends."

Like my grandfather, you have the power to change people through the stories you create. These stories can be short or long, fictional or real, but they must have one essential element: they must inspire us to change.

For example, have you ever noticed those little cards placed in hotel bathrooms? They ask guests to reuse their towels in order to save the environment, hoping guests will stop using up every single towel in the room just because fresh towel service is built into their bill. Well, the cards don't always work. However, when some hotels took a slightly different approach, the response rate doubled. The new cards noted that 50 percent of the guests staying at the hotel reused their towels. The result? Twice the amount of guests complied. When the cards stated that 50 percent of the people "who stayed in *this* room" reused their towels, the number of guests who followed suit jumped up to 75 percent. Most of us are not first adopters, but we adapt along the lines of the community we have a connection with, even if it is a hotel room that strangers have stayed in. We look to the actions of others—moved by fads, kinship, or competitiveness—to determine our own.

The hero of a story doesn't even have to be a human for us to feel empathy. We respond to any characters—be they toys, cars, robots, or even rats—that are faced with change. The characters just need to be relatable, with easily identifiable human traits.

For example, Lightning McQueen, the arrogant racecar in the movie *Cars*, is only concerned with winning the Piston Cup but finds himself stuck in Radiator Springs. There he learns the importance of friendship through the other characters he meets and discovers that the purpose of life is more than just winning. He undergoes a change from being prideful to being compassionate. He learns to care. And we care right along with him.

When Sully, the top "scarer" at Monsters Incorporated, accidentally befriends a little girl and discovers that kids aren't dangerous, toxic, or evil, we feel for Sully when he risks losing his job, his best friend, and more to save her. It's a story of courage. Sully does something out of his comfort zone because he knows it's the right thing to do, and we take that risk with him.

Pixar films have been widely successful, not because of their amazing CG animation and technical accomplishments. Although everybody marvels at the realistically animated hair, cloth, or skin (and that's important), the films are hits because they tell powerful stories with characters who undergo change. When storytellers do their job well, the characters changing in a story engender change in us, inspiring us to be more caring or courageous in our own lives. If nothing else, we become better at listening to and feeling for others who are facing changes of their own.

Great stories are not restricted to great movies or books. They are also useful tools in the business world. Like ads for jogging shoes or health products that show people successfully living healthier lives through exercising or changing their diets. Ads that inspire us to change are the result of good storytelling. Whatever the topic, whoever the audience, whether the format is short, long, or animated, storytelling can inspire and change people.

Must all stories have a happy ending to inspire people? Nope.

While most of us enjoy a happy Hollywood ending full of characters changing for the better, you can also tell stories that have darker endings. Stories like these teach us tough lessons about life, but also invite us to yearn for something better in our own lives. These tragedies and cautionary tales invite the audience to look at themselves, and say, "That could happen to me!" The *grass is greener* stories; the *I wish I could be rich* or *I wish I could be God* or *I wish I knew what all women were thinking* stories. These teach valuable lessons. Don't lie. Don't overreach. Don't engage in wishful thinking. Don't wander. Look what happens to you if you _____ (fill in the blank).

After *Toy Story* came out in 1995 and was declared a huge success, employees wondered if Pixar would try their hand at making live-action movies as well. What about TV shows? Video games? Pixar employees were prepared to make the leap from startup to a worldwide media company, like Disney. Our heads were in the clouds.

In order to keep us grounded, Steve Jobs shared with us a cautionary tale that kept us focused as a company and safe from going bankrupt. It went like this: "When Apple was just getting started, the team and I loved to go eat at one particular sandwich shop in

Silicon Valley. Although it was a small shop, owned and operated by a family, it served the very best sandwiches in town. The sandwiches were so delicious, we would even wait forty-five minutes in line just to get one. But as the sandwich shop grew in popularity, the owners began to serve coffee and pastries to compete with Starbucks and Krispy Kreme. Unfortunately, their coffee and pastries were mediocre, and the attention to detail on their trademark sandwiches lapsed. So we stopped eating there. Months later, I discovered the sandwich shop was gone. They had spread themselves too thin, and they went out of business."

Steve's story drove home the point loud and clear: Don't overleverage yourself. Even though *Toy Story* was a wild success, if we spread ourselves too thin, too fast, we would risk losing it all. We needed to focus on making really good animated family films. Steve knew the best way to communicate this message to us was by sharing a story about characters facing change and learning a lesson. This is what great storytellers and great stories do.

But whether it's a happy ending or a Greek tragedy, you must keep the characters in your stories moving through a world of peaks and pitfalls, hopes and obstacles. Whatever you do, don't let your story go static—the characters must change. Otherwise your story will lose steam out of the gate and your audience will quickly lose interest. Will Rogers said it best, "Even if you are on the right track, you'll get run over if you just sit there."

Character Arc

The change that a character undergoes is called a character arc, which is any difficult journey through fear, limitation, block, or wound. For example, at the beginning of *Toy Story*, Woody is controlling and arrogant because he fears being abandoned. By the end of the story, Woody learns to care and be content with what the future holds. This is Woody's character arc. He moves from being afraid of abandonment, through a series of outer conflicts, and arrives at being content with what the future holds. A character's arc looks like this:

1. The story starts on a normal day.
2. The character is launched into an unfamiliar world, encountering characters and obstacles that challenge their way of thinking.
3. By the end of the story the character returns to where they started, but is notably changed.

This character arc is not about events or obstacles, but how characters struggle to keep their values and passions, which are being threatened through those events and obstacles. Some things your characters may risk losing are: wealth, success, avoiding failure, friends, winning a particular competition, good grades, organization, justice, compassion, love, the environment, productivity, power, humility, and so on.

Here is another way to look at the character arc:

Who the character was / what the character learns / who the character becomes

- prideful race car / to care / compassionate race car
- insecure king / to have courage / confident king
- bad father / to care / good father
- naïve monster / to have courage / aware monster

Who is your character at the beginning? Who do they become at the end? Is your character a customer who changes because of challenges faced and overcome with the help of your product? Or did you and your team learn and grow through completing a project? Or have you been transformed by becoming a parent for the first time?

A, B, and C Stories

Stories can also show more than one character changing. Although Woody is the main character in *Toy Story*, Buzz Lightyear also changes. While Woody learns to care and become less selfish, Buzz discovers that even though he is not the "real" Buzz Lightyear but only a toy, he can still be important to his owner. Woody's character arc is the A story, while Buzz's arc is the B story. There can also be a C story, which in the case of *Toy Story* is how the other toys, Mr. Potato Head, Rex, Slinky Dog, and the others, learn to have courage during their transition moving to a new home with their owner.

- Your A story should fill up 60 percent of your story
- B story, 30 percent
- C story, 10 percent

In *Toy Story* this ratio is how it played out respectively for Woody, Buzz, and the gang of toys. Whether you are watching a movie, play, or TV show, you will see A, B, and C stories play out again and again. The trick is not to tell so many stories that you confuse the audience, or conversely, bore them by following the changes in too few. I only use an A or A and B story in short films that are thirty seconds to five minutes long, because most short stories tend to have another character on the journey with the main character. When I create a film that is fifteen minutes to ninety minutes long, I may add a C story to my A and B stories. It's just a way to keep the audience interested. When you're sharing a story in the form of a pitch, at a meeting or any other business event, flip between the arcs of your company's story and different projects, teams, or clients. This way you can keep your audience informed, intrigued, and transformed as you explore the changes played out in your A, B, and C stories. One way to toggle between stories is by having one or two partners pitch alongside you. For example, you share the story around the company (the A story), the next pitching partner shares a story around the project (the B story), and the last pitching partner shares a story around the teams or clients (the C story). Pitching in teams is a great way to keep listeners engaged and transformed while delivering lengthier pitches or presentations.

For thousands of years, great leaders in entertainment, politics, and business have used storytelling to inspire their listeners to try something new. What transformational stories can you share that will inspire people to learn about you, your company, and its products, solutions, and services?

- While a great hook catches our attention, the promise of change brings us to the edge of our seats.
- Only 15 percent of us are risk-takers or early adopters, while 85 percent of us need motivation to change.
- We inspire people to change by telling stories. A character or characters who go through a change generate empathy in the audience.
- Stories that engender change are not restricted to great movies or books. Successful businesses have used compelling stories

for years. Remember IBM's use of Chaplin's "Little Tramp" character to sell PCs?

- The change that a character undergoes is called a character arc, which is any difficult journey through fear, limitation, block, or wound.
- A character arc is not about events or obstacles, but how a character struggles to stay true to their values and passions, which are being threatened.
- Toggle between an A, B, and C story to keep your audience engaged during lengthier pitches and presentations.
- What stories can you tell that include relevant characters changing and learning? These stories can include success stories, testimonials, campaign stories, corporate histories, and personal stories.

- CHAPTER 3 -

Connecting

If a story is not about the hearer,

he will not listen.

—JOHN STEINBECK

N ot long before his death, Walt Disney made a series of short films for his executive staff. The films were shot by William High, a cameraman at the Disney Studio that had worked on *Snow White*, *Fantasia*, and many other early Disney films. The first short film was to be shown to the entire executive staff immediately after Walt's funeral. In this film Walt addressed each staff member by name and occasionally pointed to them. (They were sitting in assigned seats for the viewing.) Walt covered what was expected from each of them. There was not a dry eye in the room at the conclusion of Walt's beyond-the-grave presentation.

A series of five-minute films, made for specific staffers, were shown to them after Walt had been gone six months. A final set of short films, made for each executive, were shown at the two-year anniversary of Walt's death. Walt was a believer in the power of making authentic connections with his employees, peers, and guests—even after his death!

Which leads us to a critical question—who is your audience? Who are you trying to connect to? Are they married or single? What is their age and gender? Are they investors, clients, or fellow employees? Where are they from and where are they going? You need to know their passions, struggles, habits, and quirks. Without this information, you may create a great story, but it won't be relatable to your particular audience.

Entertainment and marketing companies spend millions of dollars researching their audiences before crafting any story or message. While you may not be spending millions of dollars on a campaign, if you don't know your audience, your efforts—whatever your budget— may be misplaced or underutilized, which in turn could affect your success. Collecting data is the best way to connect with a specific audience, revealing patterns, trends, and associations, particularly as it relates to human behavior and interactions. Shopping habits, product loyalty, along with preferences, joys, fears, beliefs, pitfalls, and dreams.

Let's examine how to effectively connect with a specific or more general audience in entertainment or business.

A few years back, the future of our long-held family toy store was thrown into doubt. After sixty years in a location in San Francisco, the landlord quadrupled the rent with the intent to kick out Jeffrey's Toys and bring in a chain store. Unable to afford the new lease, my dad had no choice but to close the last Jeffrey's Toys store in San Francisco.

A few years later, I received a call from my dad. He had discovered the perfect spot in San Francisco to open a new toy store.

"Wait a minute," I replied, "aren't you retired?" He laughed and explained how the new location was only a one-minute walk from Union Square; it had great foot traffic; it offered lots of space. But there was one major problem—the landlord had already chosen a coffee chain to move in. My dad asked if I could come up with a pitch that would be so compelling the landlord would change his mind. I had no idea what to expect, but I agreed to help.

Before I could even begin to craft a pitch, I needed to know more about the landlord. I needed to make a personal connection with him. What were his likes, dislikes, family background, age, and so on?

As it turned out, the landlord's family had been in San Francisco since the Civil War. And he had a soft spot for family history and genealogy. His grandparents and great-grandparents were Jewish. He was a collector of fine art and paintings. He also loved the diversity and culture of the city. After gathering this information on my audience, I felt prepared to meet with the landlord.

On the day of the meeting, I brought my prepared materials, including a handful of pictures. I first thanked the landlord for finding time to meet. Pointing out dozens of old family photos on the walls of his office, he noted that his family has been in San Francisco for over six generations. I was impressed. I shared that my family had been in San Francisco for almost as long, about five generations. For the next couple of minutes we happily exchanged family stories, and I shared how my great-grandfather had spent twenty-five years fixing wristwatches in San Francisco until one day his boss fired him after finding out he was Jewish. The landlord shared that his great-grandparents, who were also Jewish, had struggled as well.

The landlord asked what my great-grandfather did after being fired. Well, I replied, it was actually my great-grandmother Birdie who came up with a solution. She suggested that they open a small five-and-dime variety store. Of course, they had little money to invest with, but they managed to scrounge up enough to purchase a small shop in a poor neighborhood consisting mainly of Jewish people, and they ran the store with their two high school sons, Mannie and Joel (my grandfather and great uncle). They called the store "Birdie's Variety Store," and they sold everything from inexpensive cosmetics to pots and pans, socks, thread, greeting cards, and even some toys. But it was more than just a store. It was a place that promoted diversity in the neighborhood by eagerly serving anybody and everybody. And the little store grew.

After my grandpa Mannie and uncle Joel graduated high school, they volunteered to serve in World War II, and when they returned home they got married and had kids—just like thousands of other war veterans. And those kids wanted toys. Soon the five-and-dime store sold fewer housewares, hardware, and thread, and more toys. My family turned the small variety store into a toy store, "Birdie's Toy House."

As the demand grew for toys, so did the number of our family's toy stores, and my grandpa and great uncle helped expand from one to five, until it became the largest chain of family-run toy stores in the San Francisco Bay Area. The number of employees also grew, and my family made a point to hire employees based on their work ethic and love of toys, not on their gender, color, or religious beliefs.

As I shared the story of my family, I showed pictures of our stores, and the diverse group of employees having fun with the customers. The landlord smiled. Then the mood of the room became somber as I shared how my dad's past landlord quadrupled the rent, essentially kicking him out, and our last family-run store in San Francisco was shut down.

The landlord was moved and curious how the story would end. The shifts between highs and lows, caused by the rapid release of happy chemicals (dopamine and endorphins) and sad chemicals (oxytocin), kept him on the edge of his seat. I continued.

"Now, you have a great building," I said, "and I know that you could easily lease it to another chain coffee shop." I paused for a moment, "But does San Francisco really need another coffee shop? Wouldn't it be great to open up something that would make a difference, like a toy store that offers as much diversity and creativity as the city of San Francisco? Not only through selling toys, but also offering cartooning classes and other creative activities for kids and families. A place that makes people happy one toy at a time?" The landlord smiled.

"You know what," he said, "let's do it." He had changed his mind because I had used story to make a personal connection.

He had changed his mind because I had sold him more than a toy store. I was selling him on me, and my dad. A big part of your story or message is about *you*, who you are, your personality, your track record, your voice, your background, and your passion.

Before you prepare a message or casually deliver a story, you must define your audience. For example, when someone asks what your job entails, tailor your answer to the person, or the audience, you are addressing. If you're speaking to a fellow parent, forge a connection using your common bond of parenthood. If you don't know your audience and what really speaks to them, your story is bound to fall on deaf ears.

Don't forget to take size into account. Are you trying to inspire the six people in your business unit, the fifty people attending your sales pitch, or a thousand people viewing your website or ad?

Universal Themes

While at Pixar, I focused on creating stories that would reach as many people as possible. How would I do this? By using universal themes—based on fears and desires—that all people have in common. Universal themes connect with all genders, ages, and cultures. For example, we are all born with the fear of being abandoned. Where is Mommy? Where is Daddy? Our existence is reliant on our parents or parental figures. The *Toy Story* franchise deals with this theme of abandonment almost exclusively. Like any good protagonist, Woody wants something, and that something is love from the boy who owns him. He fears being abandoned. In the first *Toy Story*, Woody is worried about being replaced by a newer, shinier, cooler toy, Buzz Lightyear. In *Toy Story 2,* Woody is worried about getting old and being abandoned by his owner after his arm is ripped. In *Toy Story 3*, Woody's owner is eighteen and heading off to college. Woody must confront his fear of abandonment, and discover that although you can't physically be there for somebody all the time, you can be there for someone in spirit, even if they're miles away or all grown-up.

The desire for love and belonging is one of the six universal themes that have been used in storytelling for thousands of years. The six themes:

1. love and belonging
2. safety and security
3. freedom and spontaneity

4. power and responsibility
5. fun and playfulness
6. awareness and understanding

For example, in *Finding Nemo*, the main character, Marlin, desires "safety and security" for his son, Nemo, while struggling not to be overprotective.

Mr. Incredible in *The Incredibles* desires "freedom and spontaneity" from his boring job, longing to be a superhero again, while also being a good husband and father.

Lightning McQueen in *Cars* desires "power and responsibility" as he longs to win the Piston Cup, while also learning the importance of friendship and enjoying life.

Joy from *Inside Out* desires "fun and playfulness" in her life all the time, but learns that a complete life is about embracing all the different emotions, like sadness, anger, fear, and disgust.

These films connect with all genders, ages, and cultures because they engage universal themes. You, too, can use one or more of these universal themes whenever you need to connect with a broad audience.

For example, if you're marketing a car, don't create a commercial that only highlights the data and stats, but one that also tells a story with a universal theme that will connect with your audience.

Mercedes did a great job connecting with a broad audience in a recent commercial called "Snow Date" that tapped the universal theme of "safety and security." We see a dad reluctantly driving his twelve-year-old son through an awful snowstorm to a movie theater. As they drive, the dad says, "It's sure coming down." The son responds, "She'll be there." We realize the boy is going on a date. We see the Mercedes handle the bad weather like a pro. Finally, the

Mercedes safely arrives at the movie theater—but the girl isn't there. The boy's heartbroken, tapping into the universal themes of "love, belonging, and abandonment." The dad consoles his son and together they walk back to the Mercedes. Off on the horizon, we see another car approaching the movie theater through the snowstorm. It's the girl, and she's arrived in a Mercedes. The two tweens exchange a shy "hello" and enter the movie theater.

Sometimes you will use one universal theme in a story, other times multiple universal themes. You also need to continuously revisit your audience, assessing their concerns, because people's passions and struggles change, along with trends, and the themes you use must change accordingly.

Know Your Audience

Ten years after Disneyland opened, Walt Disney discovered that he had a problem—attendance was dropping. But why? Demographics. The kids who had been coming to Disney for years were growing up. They were now teenagers, and their interests had changed. They saw the Magic Kingdom as a place only for little kids. Disney asked his teenage daughter Dianne, "What would get you to come to Disneyland?" Her one-word answer, "Boys." A lightbulb went off in Walt Disney's head. Until then, nothing resembling a nightlife had existed at Disney. That's what the teenagers wanted. They wanted music and dancing—nightlife. So Walt Disney brought in bands and dancing and created "Disneyland after Dark." It doubled attendance at the park. He even made a documentary about it. Walt Disney never stopped trying to connect to his audience and insisted that none of his company executives at Disneyland work in a bubble. "I don't want you guys sitting behind desks," he'd say. "I want you out in the park, watching what people are doing and finding out how you can make the place more enjoyable for them."

Connecting with your audience doesn't mean reducing inspiration to a science or formula. It's a matter of carefully observing people and finding new sources of inspiration. Remember: there is always room to make a stronger connection.

At Pixar, we would collect data by setting up audience previews, showing prerelease versions of our films so we could learn if we were effectively connecting with people. Do they know who the main character is? What the main character wants? What the theme of the story is? We listened and then made changes according to their comments and feedback, which helped us as filmmakers improve our story.

At the same time, we didn't want the audience's reactions to inhibit new ideas. An audience may request more explosions, but ninety minutes of explosions will drive everyone out of the theater. In short, don't let feedback stifle your progress or hold you back from innovation.

Research trips are another great way to collect data to connect with your audience and discover the heart of your story or message. For the first *Cars* movie, we needed to know about the history of Route 66, because the location was going to play a big part in our story. It is an iconic roadway, a monument to the early history of motorized travel and the American expansion westward. Who lives there? What is life like? What was it like? How has it changed? The best way to learn about it was in person, so our story team packed up and headed to the Southwest for two weeks. We needed to discover the emotional juice of Route 66, and how we could tap into it.

It was the middle of summer—dry, hot, blinding sun. I was stuck in a car with my coworkers. I wanted to be home with my family. But during the course of our trip, we met people who would inspire the characters in *Cars*, including Mater and Sally. We explored locations on the Mother Road that inspired Radiator Springs, the Cozy Cone, and Flo's Diner. By the end of the trip, the most important discovery we made was about ourselves. Life is more than just reaching a destination. Life is about the journey. While striving to make the best movies at Pixar, we had forgotten to enjoy the ride. It's the difficulties, surprises, left turns, and time taken to slow down and look around that bring you closer to true meaning and the things that make life worthwhile. We had discovered the theme and emotional juice for *Cars*, along with rediscovering ourselves along the way.

A research trip can inspire you in unplanned ways. We found the data we were looking for on that trip, but we found a whole lot more, and it shows up in the story and characters of *Cars*.

Pixar's *Inside Out* proved to be an even more challenging research project. The story team couldn't travel inside the mind of a twelve-year-old girl to explore what universal emotions drove her decisions. Instead, psychiatrists, psychologists, neurologists and other experts were brought into the studio to help. A story about the inner workings of emotions had to be grounded in scientific truth, while also connecting with the audience.

Making that effort to truly connect with your audience, whether broad or specific, will always pay off in building better brands, companies, products, and relationships.

- You may have an amazing hook and characters who face change, but if the audience can't relate to your story, they won't listen or care.

- To connect with a broad audience, you must use universal themes that relate to fear and desire.
- Connecting with your audience doesn't mean reducing inspiration to a formula. It is an exercise in looking, observing, and relating.
- Collecting data remains a great way to reveal patterns, trends, and associations, particularly as it relates to human behavior and interactions.
- Who is your audience? Who are the people at the heart of your message?
- When was the last time you went on a research trip?

- CHAPTER 4 -

Authenticity

Tell me the facts and I'll learn.
Tell me the truth and I'll believe.
But tell me a story and it will live
in my heart forever.

–Native American Proverb

Be warned—while I've laid out some of the basic principles of storytelling in the first few chapters, without authenticity woven into your story, your message will lack the magic that moves people to engage with you and your company.

The hard truth is that when you create stories without heart—by which I mean *your heart*—your audience feels *manipulated* not *moved*. They become suspicious, thinking they are being tricked into buying something rather than being inspired. Respect your audience. Create stories and experiences that deal in honest emotions without being overtly manipulative.

So how can you create authentic stories that build strong bonds with your audience? The answer is don't be clever. Be vulnerable and honest.

I know it's hard. We're programmed from an early age to believe that being vulnerable and taking chances is socially risky, that we are setting ourselves up to fail or be ridiculed. But being vulnerable is at the center, the very heart, of storytelling. Vulnerability creates the strongest connection possible with an audience. It makes you and your story relatable. Human. Authentic. Believable.

We connect so much better to people when their "humanness" is on full display. We cannot relate to perfection. Allowing yourself and characters in your stories to be vulnerable to an audience creates empathy and authenticity. When sharing with others what your company is about, or your role within the company, or the products or solutions you provide, don't forget to share the obstacles you have faced along with the successes. When people feel connected to your humanity, they can really begin to root for you.

Ups and downs, highs and lows, twists and turns, positives and negatives. They all work together to make an interesting, and ultimately, enthralling story. A lot of us hesitate to be real, because we believe that people—clients and future customers—will see our flaws and mistakes as a sign of weakness, but it's actually quite the opposite.

Recently I worked with a group of salespeople at a financial institution. I asked them to write down how they landed their current job. I was amazed at how few included setbacks or struggles of any kind, and of course, all of the personal stories were snoozers. So I dug in deeper, asking them if they had *any* struggles along their journey. After much prying, one woman shared how she had to work as a waitress at a dumpy steakhouse to make her way through college. Another employee shared how he had developed ulcers the first couple of years at his job trying to get a promotion. Another woman shared how she juggled raising two kids on her own while working full-time. By getting "real" these people suddenly became likable and authentic to their peers and managers.

In the 1960s, the Avis car rental company was having a difficult time competing with Hertz, the number one rental car company in the United States. Being a smaller fish in the rental car pond, Avis developed a revolutionary ad campaign. They put out an ad that stated, "When you're only No. 2, you try harder. Or else." Below the headline was a drawing of a little scared fish swimming away from a big fish. Avis was being vulnerable and honest. Communicating a message that they will work harder than their competitors to get and keep your business. Because without working hard, they would simply be gobbled up by the bigger fish. Was admitting they were number two a stupid move? Not at all. They created empathy in their audience. We root for the underdogs, especially if we know they are persistent and will never give up. And yes, after the ad ran for a year,

Avis became the number one car rental agency in America. Customers wanted to help Avis become number one.

Next time you give a presentation, lead a board meeting, or deliver a pitch, use personal anecdotes and reflections drawn from your own experiences that show you are vulnerable. CEOs and leaders and salespeople of all kinds often forget that this is what makes a great leader and/or hero. It's not only about strength or raw talent but also being human and authentic. It's not perfection that creates likability and authenticity, but instead, vulnerability and persistence.

Being vulnerable is very different from being self-deprecating. I have witnessed many speakers share their shortcomings, bad memory, small stature, or other personal failings. This is not being vulnerable; it's putting yourself down. An audience wants to be on your side. But they won't root for you if you play the martyr and belittle yourself. Instead share how you tried something new, failed, and learned.

Steve Jobs was very open about his failures, but he followed up his stories with a success based upon what he'd learned. We knew that any time we failed at Pixar, he would encourage us to get up and try again. This is how we all learned to go beyond our limits. In essence, Steve was selling a philosophy to us, and it made us all better in the process. That was perhaps the core of his leadership technique, and he did it naturally. He was authentic.

Memory Prompts

It is worth repeating a thousand times that the key to creating authentic stories is not to be clever, but instead to be honest and share what you know and feel. Your life and personal experiences, and the way you relate to them are the best material you have when it comes to developing authentic experiences. I know you can't remember every moment of your life, but you can summon many memories by prompting yourself.

Start with a memory. Write down or draw the things that pop up into your head as you focus on that memory.

Let's say you call on your earliest memory of being in a car. Suddenly, an image pops into your head, and you start unlocking other images connected to that car; images that have been stored away inside your subconscious for years. Write those memories down. Those memories can prompt new ideas for a great story or a moment in a story that communicates a lesson, message, or takeaway connected to a facet of your company or a product/solution.

Other prompts for authentic stories could include

- What was your bravest moment?
- What was your most embarrassing moment?
- When did you first experience the value of teamwork?

You can make lists like this for yourself. They can help surface moments and memories that have been buried for years.

You can go further and develop prompts specifically tailored to an idea; your first car, for example. Imagine that car and answer these questions:

Where are you?
Are you inside or outside of the car?
If you're inside, which seat are you in?
What are you doing?
What time of day is it?
Why are you there?

Authenticity

Who else is with you?
How old are you?

I remember the first car I was in as a kid. It was our toy store's white van with the Jeffery's Toys logo painted on both sides. How might I respond to the prompts?

Where are you?
Movie theater parking lot.

Are you inside or outside of the car?
Inside the van.

If you're inside, which seat are you in?
Sitting on a wooden chair between the driver seat and passenger seat.

What are you doing?
About to jump to hyperdrive.

What time of day is it?
Before noon.

Why are you there?
I just saw Star Wars for the first time.

Who else is with you?
My dad.

How old are you?
Five years old.

Just like that, I started with an image that evolved into a story with relatable characters and drama. A simple prompt unlocked a memory of seeing *Star Wars* with my dad for the very first time.

I remember we were so moved by the movie that my dad stepped on the gas pedal of our van to simulate jumping into hyperdrive. The wooden chair I was sitting on flipped backwards and I slammed my head on the back of the van door. Yes, I was sitting on an unsecured wooden chair in a van with no seatbelt. It was the '70s and people didn't worry about these things.

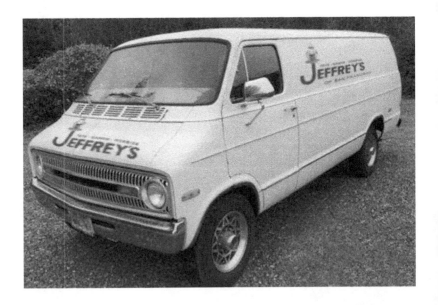

Entire movies have been written based on memories. *A Christmas Story* is based on Jean Shepherd's book *In God We Trust: All Others*

Pay Cash. The book was comprised of short stories originally published in the 1960s that dealt with Shepherd's childhood growing up in Indiana in the 1940s. Yes, there really was a Red Ryder cowboy rifle and a sexy leg lamp in his childhood.

Finding Nemo is based on the director's own experience of being an overprotective first-time father. John Lasseter was projecting his own busy life and the need to slow down and enjoy the journey while creating *Cars*. Why did he choose cars? His father was a mechanic. Pixar never optioned scripts or purchased book rights. Every one of the tales we wove, we developed in-house, and they always came from a personal place.

With *Inside Out*, the director Pete Docter found a way to relate some of his own story into the movie. Pete, not only the tallest animator I have ever met, but also the happiest, has a happy wife and happy kids. His family is so happy, that it almost makes you feel guilty for not being happier yourself. But then everything changed when his daughter Ellie turned twelve. She wasn't happy all the time. All of a sudden she spent more time being sad, scared, disgusted, and angry than happy.

Pete didn't know what to do. He tried to be even happier to offset his daughter's sadness, but that didn't work. They took more family vacations to Disneyland, but that didn't work either. Her sadness could not be squashed, muted, or balanced out. In the end, Pete realized that it was okay for her to be sad. That all the emotions in life are necessary to be a well-rounded person. He was able to translate this personal experience with his daughter into the story of *Inside Out*. It was simple enough, because he allowed himself to go to a vulnerable place to tell a story that everyone could identify with.

The most successful companies and brands don't merely promote good ideas, they promote ideas they are passionate about, and have a personal investment in. If you follow the path of your sincerest passion, where would it take you? When you really acknowledge what you love in life, the thing that you truly want to do, you are driven to make something authentic and personal, as opposed to something for only financial gain or attention. Steve Jobs said, "Being the richest man in the cemetery doesn't matter to me. Going to bed at night saying we've done something wonderful . . . that's what matters to me."

The Feeling Is the Message

So you need to be vulnerable and honest to create authentic stories, but you must also exercise restraint when delivering your message. Sentimental not saccharine. If you hammer home the conclusion you want the audience to reach too overtly, your story will feel preachy or moralistic.

Let your audience discover the message on their own. "I want to give the audience a hint of a scene," said Orson Welles. "No more than that. Give them too much and they won't contribute anything themselves. Give them just a suggestion, and you get them working with you. That's what gives the theater meaning: when it becomes a social act."

All of the films and TV shows I've worked on have taught me to carefully guard against telling audiences the moral of the story. That kills the authenticity of the experience. The moral in *Finding Nemo* was more or less, "Being overprotective won't lead your loved ones to a better life. Life has to take its course and you have to learn to let go." But we would never have a character say that to the audience. Instead, we communicated the moral of *Finding Nemo* in a way that wasn't belittling, respecting the autonomy of the audience and our relationship with them. We gave the messenger job to Dory, who dispatched sage advice to Marlin (Nemo's father) in a much softer, relational way. Dory essentially told Marlin, "If you never let anything happen to Nemo, nothing will ever happen to him." As the audience, we appreciate the moment. We hear the moral, but we don't feel talked down to.

As Frank Capra said, "I made mistakes in drama. I thought drama was when actors cried. But drama is when the audience cries."

The trick, if you can call it that, is having people discover the moral on their own. If you do it right it feels more like solving a puzzle than being told something, because each person arrives at the solution in his or her own unique way. You only provide the right clues.

Think of your idea and your audience as two electrodes. If they touch, the current passes from one to the other in a very efficient and unseen way. But if you place the electrodes close together, but not touching, you get a spark . . . and it's the spark of understanding that moves your audience. Their spark, not yours.

The moral of a story is akin to a company's mission statement. Instead of inflicting another boring mission statement on the world, choose one to three words along with visuals that represent what you want people to *feel* when they encounter your products or services. Tiffany & Company does an excellent job communicating its mission statement through the colors, typeface, and images used in their ads, on their website, on packaging, and in their stores. These elements are chosen carefully to create the feeling of "elegance, escape, love." That's what they want you to feel. They want you to experience the joy of discovery through the narrative and visual storytelling. This is what great companies do.

As a kid raised on all things Disney, I never once heard a mission statement about their products. Like millions of other people, I was simply entertained and delighted once inside the Disneyland theme parks, the stores, or watching a Disney movie. Authentic mission statements are not said but felt.

My parents and grandparents created an authentic experience that communicated "play and fun" in their toy stores by setting up slot-car tracks, areas to read books, and spaces to build model kits with friends. They wanted to create a feeling, not a mission statement.

Strive to create authentic stories, warts and all. Stories that are vulnerable and honest, with characters that are likable and relatable. Build a stronger relationship with your audience by inviting them to an experience, not a mission statement. Because in the end, people will forget what you said or what you did, but they will never forget how you made them feel.

- Use empathy and authenticity to create a strong emotional bond with your audience. Once your story falls short of any credibility, empathy soon dissipates and your film, book, song, or pitch loses the heart of your listener or viewer.
- Be honest. Share your own experiences, not just your successes but your struggles and failures as well. It can be difficult, but vulnerability is the heart of storytelling.
- Persistence is better than success. If you don't fail now and again, you aren't innovating.
- Allow your audience to discover the message and meaning of your story on their own.
- Authentic mission statements are not said but felt.

- Choose one to three words that represent what you want people to feel when they encounter your products or services. How would you draw those feelings out of readers with narrative and visual storytelling?

- **CHAPTER 5** -

Story Structure

If the story is good, the picture may be good, but if the story is weak, good color, top actors, music, and animation cannot save it.

—WALT DISNEY

From Homer to Shakespeare to Spielberg, great storytellers have all paid attention to story structure, and you should too. Stories with a beginning, a middle, and an end are universal, crossing all borders and nationalities, ages and genders, regardless of status or class. Why? It's simply because everything in our world operates on a beginning, middle, and end cycle.

For example, the sun rises, gives light to the day, and then gives way to night. We are born, live, and die. We see flowers sprout, bloom, and one day fade. These cycles of a beginning, middle, and end are all around us and inspire the stories we tell. It's instinctive, and an essential part of who we are. Every aspect of the human experience confirms it.

Whether you are creating a ninety-minute film, with an act 1, 2, and 3, or a thirty-minute sales pitch, you need to have a clear beginning, middle, and end, or you'll run the risk of boring, confusing, or frustrating your audience.

The three-part story structure is also referred to as the *setup, build,* and *payoff.*

When Steve Jobs introduced the iPhone in 2007, his pitch followed the beginning (setup), middle (build), and end (payoff) cycle like this:

Setup: Steve, the hero in the story, shared how he created something to solve the ordinary-world problem of poorly made smartphones. He even claimed that all smartphones on the market were dumb.

Build: Steve showed how his smartphone was smarter than all of our home computers, along with sharing the obstacles and struggles that went into creating the iPhone and how he and his team solved these problems, like replacing a clunky stylus pen with a multitouch screen and difficult-to-install applications with "apps."

Payoff: By the end of the pitch, Steve had demonstrated how his new iPhone was going to change the ordinary world of smartphones. The audience was excited and inspired.

In the beginning/setup of a story, you create "the ordinary world," which includes you or your hero in their natural environment. At this point the audience needs to learn about the hero's passion. You must also introduce a problem that disrupts the ordinary world enough to force the hero to come up with a solution.

The middle/build of the story involves finding that solution. This includes the ups and downs, the obstacles and struggles that your hero experiences on the way to finding the solution.

The end/payoff of the story is sharing how you or your hero succeeded, in a way that excites and inspires your audience.

The Six Story Stages

Once you get acclimated with the cycle of setup, build, and payoff, you can dive in deeper. In filmmaking, we break setup, build, and payoff down into six "story stages":

- Exposition
- Inciting Incident
- Progressive Complications
- Crisis
- Climax
- Resolution

Exposition

The exposition is the setup of your story. This is where you share the ordinary world by showing the Who, What, Why, and Where.

- Who is the main character?
- What do they want?
- Why do they want it?
- Where does the story take place?

Without this information, your audience has no point of reference and will be lost from the very beginning.

What does your main character want? What passion or desire drives them? It could be becoming a fighter pilot, a professional hockey player, or a snake charmer. Indiana Jones's great passion is rescuing archaeological items, whereas WALL-E is a hopelessly romantic robot who just wants to find true love and companionship. The passion can be anything; but you must set it up at the beginning.

For balance, just as your character has a desire, they should also have flaws. A flaw is a limitation, imperfection, phobia, or deficiency that's present in a character who may otherwise be highly functional. Low self-esteem can be a flaw, as well as a severe case of vanity, or even a fear of heights. We all have character flaws, and they make us fascinating and unique, so you should never hesitate to include them in the characters you create.

Once the essential groundwork has been laid out in your exposition, it's time to pull the rug out from underneath the main character—and the audience—and set the story into motion. To do this, you need to introduce a life-changing event.

Inciting Incident

This is the part of your story where you take that one thing that your protagonist is most passionate about and turn it completely upside down, either by taking away what they most desire or giving it to them. In *The Incredibles*, the hero's passion is taken away from him when he's no longer allowed to be a superhero. Conversely, the main character in the movie *Big* is a little boy who wants to grow up overnight, and one day his wish is granted.

Either way, the inciting incident takes the main character's passion and uses it to drive the story. If done right, the audience will feel sympathetic toward the main character and will want to see how the protagonist will change or adapt to their new, unexpected situation. This is when the story gets *really* interesting; progressively so.

Progressive Complications

The progressive complications are exactly what they sound like; complications that get progressively more complex as we follow the main character through the story. Through the progressive complications, we see the trials that the protagonist must endure as they either try to put their life back together after their passion has been taken away from them, or try to adapt to their wish having been granted. The protagonist goes through most of his or her changes during these progressive complications. It is important to remember that these changes, this learning experience, must happen in stages, and the severity of each complication must increase if you are to keep the audience engaged. As such, the first complication will be the easiest to overcome, and the last will be the hardest.

From a purely entertainment perspective, you want to ramp up your complications from level one to ten to keep the audience's interest. If you start at a level five intensity and then drop down to a two, people will get bored. Like us, the main character will take the path of least resistance when it comes to facing changes or adapting to situations. Eventually the main character will reach level ten and will be faced with the ultimate *crisis* decision to make.

Crisis

The crisis decision is that fork in the road where the main character must choose to act on the lessons learned throughout the story, or turn their back on them. Will the character stay the same broken person they were at the beginning of the story, or will they choose to change? At this point the audience is in a trance, sitting on the edge of their seats, hoping and praying that the character will make the right choice. On some level, we believe that if the main character can make the right choice, then we can overcome the struggles in our own lives and change for the better.

In many stories, the crisis moment is motivated by a *mantra*. A mantra can be a saying, an image, a memory, or something that the heroes read, remember, or reflect on in the course of their journey. No matter how it is represented, the mantra compels the main character to reflect on what they've learned. Almost every movie has a mantra, whether stated or not, at this crisis stage of the story. In *Star Wars* the mantra is "Use the Force," and in *Ratatouille* it is, "Anyone can cook."

If the main character in your story does decide to change, then this type of story generally has a positive ending. Movies like *Finding Nemo* end on a positive note with the main characters changing. But if the protagonist refuses to change at the crisis moment, then this type of story becomes a cautionary tale with a tragic ending.

The end of the crisis moment marks the point where we move to the height of the story's intensity.

Climax

The climax of a story is when we get to see our newly changed character face and defeat their *antagonist,* or the *villain.* This is the payoff. The previous stages in the story have all led up to this point, so it should be, hands down, the most exciting and action-packed moment of the story. The important thing worth noting here is that when the protagonist overcomes their crisis moment, it's almost as if their greatest weakness has become their greatest strength. Unlike at the beginning of the story, the hero is now fully equipped to defeat the antagonist. In story terms, this is HUGE!

If the antagonist is defeated at the climax of the story, it's essential that the protagonist is the one responsible for serving up the final blow. You don't want to take this away from the hero or the audience, who by now have become totally invested in the main character. If you sidestep their moment of victory, the story will feel hollow and the audience deflated. You also need to make sure that your main character is only able to defeat the antagonist *after* their crisis decision. I've seen stories make the mistake of putting the climax before the crisis (or ignoring the crisis altogether), and it leaves the audience feeling very unsatisfied.

With the antagonist defeated or removed, our final stage kicks in.

Resolution

The resolution is like the tail end of an exciting roller-coaster ride. The coaster has come full circle, finally gliding into the station to drop us off where the ride began. The resolution of your story does the same. Our hearts are beating fast. We feel exhilarated. We can hardly believe what we have just experienced.

The resolution should tie up any loose ends so that the audience isn't left with lots of questions. This includes neatly wrapping up all the various story threads of the supporting characters. In a romantic comedy, we might see the groom's best friend finally find true love. In an action film, the villain might be hauled off to jail and the cop reunited with his father. In *Star Wars*, Han Solo receives a medal from Princess Leia.

The point is that the resolution resolves any remaining issues. It makes the terrible reality that "the story must end" a bearable one, even warming our hearts as it drops us off at the station. A good resolution leaves the audience feeling happy and satisfied with the end of the story, even if it's a sad one.

The great thing about this kind of story structure is that it's so versatile. I've personally used the six stages to develop movies, TV specials, shorts films, and a multitude of other projects. These six stages of story structure really work.

The Story Spine

Yes, the six stages of story structure can be intimidating, especially at first. This is why I encourage people to get their feet wet by starting with the "story spine." The story spine is a quick and easy way to create great stories out of thin air. This tool was first introduced to me about fifteen years ago while I was performing with the Pixar improv group, the Improvables.

Here's how it works . . .

You're given eight incomplete sentences, and all you have to do is fill in the blanks with the characters and situations, and PRESTO!

You have a well-structured story! Just make sure you don't kill off the main character at the beginning or midway through . . . that would really throw things out of whack.

The incomplete story spine looks like this:

Once upon a time . . .
And every day . . .
Until one day . . .
And because of that . . .
And because of that . . .
And because of that . . .
Until finally . . .
And since that day . . .

Here's how the story spine and the six stages of story structure correlate:

Once upon a time . . . . Exposition
And every day . . . . Exposition
Until one day . . . . Inciting Incident
Because of that . . . . Progressive Complications
Because of that . . . . Progressive Complications
Because of that . . . . Progressive Complications
Until finally . . . . Crisis and Climax
And since that day . . . . Resolution

You might find that using the story spine feels familiar. That's not surprising really, as this was one of the first ways we used to tell stories when we were kids, starting with "Once upon a time . . ."

To see this tool in practice, let's apply it to *Finding Nemo*:

Once upon a time a fish called Marlin lost his wife and all but one of his children to a barracuda attack. Marlin vowed that he would never again let anything bad happen to his only remaining son, Nemo, who had survived the attack but was left with a damaged fin.

And every day Marlin would protect Nemo from the dangers of the ocean. But Marlin was overprotective and held Nemo back from having fun and even from going to school because of his damaged fin.

Until one day Nemo swam to the surface and was captured by scuba divers.

And because of that Marlin went in search of the scuba diver's boat. He met a forgetful fish named Dory who knew the scuba diver's address.

And because of that they swam to Sydney to find Nemo. On their journey, they faced sharks, jellyfish, and other dangers of the ocean.

And because of that Dory was injured and Marlin had to rescue her.

Until finally they found Nemo, but it was too late, he was dead. Marlin was crushed, and he and Dory went their separate ways. But Nemo wasn't actually dead, he had faked his death to escape! Nemo went in search of his dad and met Dory. When Nemo and Dory found Marlin, the three fish were caught in a net with hundreds of others. But Nemo knew how to escape. Marlin had to trust his son and when he did, all the fish were set free.

And since that day Marlin let his son live life to its fullest, even though the ocean is a dangerous place.

You can use this story spine exercise to share

- the story of a person. (This can be your story or the story of a founder of a company.)
- the story of a company.
- the story of how a person's future could be changed for the better if they engage with you and your company.
- the story of how a person or group of people was affected in a positive way through your company, a product, or a service you provided.

Here is an example of how you can use the story spine to tell your story or the story of a founder of a company:

Walt Disney

Once upon a time in 1901, a boy named Walter Elias Disney was born, the fourth child of a poor family living in Chicago, Illinois, that believed in hard work and tough discipline.

And every day after Walt delivered newspapers, completed his schoolwork, and finished his chores, he enjoyed drawing cartoons.

Until one day a school friend introduced him to the world of vaudeville and motion pictures, and it changed his life.

And because of that while still in high school, Walt enrolled in Saturday drawing classes at the Kansas City Art Institute and correspondence courses in cartooning.

And because of that he pursued a career as a cartoonist, which led to him directing a number of animated cartoon shorts, which were unfortunately stolen from him because of his naïveté about the world of business and copyrights.

And because of that he joined forces with his business-savvy brother, Roy, and together they were able to protect and keep creative control of all of the characters and stories created at the Walt Disney Company.

Until finally he created Mickey Mouse, which became wildly successful, the first sound cartoon "Steamboat Willie," and the first animated feature film ever, *Snow White*, in 1937.

And since that day the Walt Disney Company has become one of the most recognized and loved brands throughout the world, creating animated and live-action films and theme parks that entertain and delight audiences of all ages.

You can also use the story spine to tell a company's story:

Wente Vineyards

Once upon a time in 1883, a poor German immigrant, C. H. Wente, made the voyage to America with the dream of creating a better life.

And every day after studying winemaking under Charles Krug in Napa Valley, he immediately knew he had discovered a passion and focus amongst the vineyards.

Until one day C. H. learned about land for sale in the Livermore Valley. Recognizing that the warm days, cool nights, and gravelly soils of the valley were ideal for growing wine grapes, he and his new bride, Barbara Trautwein, purchased 47 acres there and started their own winery.

And because of that C. H. and Barbara worked hard and turned their original 47 acres of land into 200 acres of thriving vineyards. To his seven children C. H. was a father who emphasized hard work, but as he would say, "Work made life sweet." Then out of the blue, Prohibition hit.

And because of that the winery struggled. Prohibition was eventually repealed, but the family had to rebuild the business. C. H.'s sons, Ernest and Herman Wente, took over and began prominently featuring the family's name on the label—Wente Bros. Ernest was the farmer, who focused on improving quality by importing rootstock and implementing better vineyard management techniques and winemaking practices. His work with the Wente Chardonnay would earn the family the title of California's First Family of Chardonnay™. His brother Herman was the businessman with a vision of reviving America's love of wine, which most people had forgotten during Prohibition.

And because of that the winery prospered, and the brothers welcomed Karl L. Wente, the third generation of Wente winegrowers, into the business. Karl quickly took charge of the winery, working alongside his father and uncle. But uncertain of the future effects of urbanization in the Livermore Valley, and knowing he needed to sustain the family's winegrowing legacy, he looked for other regions that could grow high-quality wine grapes. In 1963, he discovered Arroyo Seco in Monterey, a rugged region with long, cool growing seasons, loamy soils, and close proximity to quality water. The area clearly had great potential, but no matter how promising it was, establishing a new wine region is always an arduous process. Nevertheless, he made the decision to purchase 300 acres of apricot orchards from Alfred Riva and eventually replanted the property in vines. The site is now home to Wente's Riva Ranch Single Vineyard Chardonnay and Pinot Noir.

Until finally the fourth generation of Wentes, Eric, Philip, and Carolyn, grew up learning everything they needed to know about the vineyards. This is a large part of what defines the Wente family legacy—generation after generation, they taught each other and benefited from the experiences of their predecessors. They built a place in the wine world by learning and cultivating what came before them.

And since that day the fifth-generation Wente winemaker, Karl D. Wente, pays homage to his family legacy by crafting a great portfolio of wines that are 100 percent estate grown and certified sustainable. "To me, I'm proud that my family has been committed to the soil and climate of Livermore Valley for five generations and Arroyo Seco since the 1960s, and that we have always had a philosophy of delivering thoughtfully balanced, food-friendly wine, with a sense of place."

Here is an example of using the story spine to communicate how a person's future could be changed for the better if they engage with you and your company:

Fictional Autonomous Car Company

Once upon a time the horseless carriage—aka the automobile—was invented, promising faster and more efficient travel regionally and nationally for work, family, sightseeing, and more.

And every day more cars were built, more cars were sold, more roads were paved, more people depended on cars, and more companies used vehicles to transport all kinds of things—even more cars! New technologies increased the speed and reliability of the automobiles, and the world became a more connected place.

Until one day the world had too many cars, resulting in traffic jams, toxic emissions, and accidents. In 2013, 1.25 million people died in car accidents worldwide. There were 32,675 accidents in the

United States alone, and 94 percent of the crashes were caused by human error. Something needed to be done.

And because of that scientists, and engineers, and great minds from all fields went to work to find solutions.

And because of that computer technologies and software began to emerge, supporting and supplementing self-managed driving functions that could eliminate human-error tragedies like drunk driving, distracted driving, and fatigue behind the wheel.

And because of that other obstacles and challenges have been addressed like government regulations, auto insurance, and building trust with the general public that self-driving vehicles can be safe.

Until finally [company name] successfully built and tested [product], bringing self-driving technology to a new high and promising improved safety and mobility.

And since that day we at [company name] will continue to push the boundaries of self-driving vehicles to provide safer, faster, and easier ways for people and products to travel from point A to point B.

Here is the last story spine example. It shows how to use the prompts to tell a story around a person or group of people inspired in a positive way through a company, a product, or service:

Jeffrey's Toys
Once upon a time my great-grandfather and great-grandmother were minding the family variety store.

And every day they would provide a variety of items to different customers.

Until one day a woman came in who was panic-stricken. The woman's husband was about to go on a very important job interview, but his suit coat was missing a button. She needed a particular button to match the others, and fast!

And because of that my great-grandparents went through the buttons on all the racks trying to help the woman find a match. But they couldn't find a match.

And because of that my great-grandparents searched through the back storage room to find more buttons. But still couldn't find a match.

And because of that they dumped out all of the jars of buttons on the counter to see if she could identify the kind of button she needed. But they still couldn't find a match!

Until finally the woman suddenly said, "There! That's the button I need! It looks exactly like that!" She was pointing to the button on my great-grandfather's jacket. Without missing a beat he grabbed a pair of scissors, cut the button off, and handed it to her free of charge.

And since that day the customer and her family continued to shop at my great-grandparents' variety store and told all their friends.

It's sometimes hard to come up with the perfect story to illustrate the point you want to make, whether in an ad, a sales pitch, or a board meeting presentation, especially when you are under a deadline. One technique is to have a bunch of stories "on file" that you can draw from when you need one. When you have time and are relaxed, write down some important moments from your life using the story spine. Then group your stories into different categories according to themes, like coming of age, self-sacrifice, and overcoming the odds. When you want to enhance a pitch or a presentation, just make sure you choose a story that shares the same theme as your content. For example, if your content theme is overcoming the odds in business, then choose the story about the time you learned how to dance, or mastered a new language, or asked that special somebody on a date. Or if you want

to encourage a group of colleagues on the importance of teamwork, share the time you built a clubhouse with your childhood buddies, or won a game because you worked together as a team, or did a better job parenting with the help of your spouse. Your personal stories are a great way to inspire and impact your listener while still delivering the important facts and figures.

- Everything in our human experience operates on a beginning, middle, and end cycle.
- Whether you are creating a ninety-minute film or a thirty-second sales pitch, you need to have a set up, build, and payoff.
- In the beginning of a story the "the ordinary world" shows your hero in their natural environment. Your character should have a clear desire, and they should also have flaws.
- An inciting incident, or hook, takes the one thing your protagonist is most passionate about and turns it completely upside down.
- The middle of the story involves searching for the solution to the main problem, through ups and downs.
- The end of the story shows your hero succeeding, in a way that gets your audience excited and inspired.
- The story spine is a quick and easy way to create great stories out of thin air.

- CHAPTER 6 -

Heroes and Leaders

*A hero is an ordinary individual
who finds the strength to persevere
and endure in spite of
overwhelming obstacles.*

—**CHRISTOPHER REEVE, AKA SUPERMAN**

am related to some great storytellers. As far back as I can remember, my dad, mom, and other family members have always told stories. Along with tales of the toy stores, they shared the adventures of my great-grandpa Danny, who bootlegged liquor in the 1920s and worked alongside infamous gangster Bugsy Siegel. They shared the stories of my free-spirited uncle Jeff, who "easy-ridered" his way through the 1970s, snapping photos of rebellions and wars for news magazines. They told more somber stories, of my grandpa Mannie fighting as a Marine during WWII in Okinawa and my mother's postwar life growing up in war-torn Germany. All were amazing tales, and although the stories were very different, they all had two things in common. They all had a beginning, middle, and end, and presented a hero on a journey. In chapter 5 we discussed the importance of structure in storytelling; now let's talk about why and how we include heroes and leaders in our stories.

Heroes have always been present in and central to storytelling, inspiring kids and grown-ups alike through their vision, bravery, and self-sacrifice. We find heroes in the first stories told by humans in every culture, location, and language. In cave drawings dating back tens of thousands of years, we see heroic men pursuing huge beasts, putting their lives in jeopardy to feed the tribe. The very first written stories from ancient Sumeria, over four thousand years old, tell us about Gilgamesh, a man who fights evil, becomes corrupted by his greed and search for immortality, and eventually redeems himself. In these early stories we recognize the universal structure—beginning, middle, and end—but they also give us a hero, Gilgamesh, going through a transformation. It's logical to assume that these stories are quite old, having been passed on in an oral tradition for many generations before they were inscribed upon clay tablets.

So heroes have always been with us. But why?

No matter our origins, we all see ourselves as the main character of our own life. It's an important part of our human psyche. Just as we share the same set of organs, instincts, impulses, conflicts, and fears, we also all see ourselves on a personal journey through the beginning, middle, and end of our lives. No matter what culture or time in history we're born into, we have always cast ourselves as the heroes, in our own stories; our own lives.

Sometimes we tell short stories, like a trip to the dentist or winning a race; sometimes the stories are longer, like what it was like growing up in our hometown or being a parent.

From birth to death, our experiences in this life, in this mind and this body, are what make us unique. This is why the hero as a story vehicle resonates so deeply with us. We connect to the hero journey, because it is familiar, and in fact is a mirror and metaphor of our own journey, or the one that we would like to take.

To wrap my head around this idea, I think of the movie *The Truman Show*. Jim Carrey portrays a man, Truman, who lives in a world where he *is* the hero; all the other people in his world are actors, whose sole purpose is to support him. I think we all feel this way from time to time, as though *we're* the hero in the movie that is our life. So when we read a book or watch a movie, we want to be able to connect with a hero on a journey, because this is something we can all relate to.

The hero is the primary character in storytelling, often referred to as the protagonist. While the protagonist may behave as a "hero" in the context of the narrative, this is not always the case, and in fact, we can see that in the word's origin. In Greek, *protagonist* means "first fighter" (leading fighter, main fighter) involved in a struggle, or "one in agony." When considered in this light, whether the protagonist is a hero or a scoundrel is irrelevant. In fact, the ancient Greeks venerated great warriors as heroes no matter which side they fought on. Heroes are the vessel that we use to tell a story. The hero's struggles and movements, and their point of view, reflect the egocentric reality of our own lives because we only truly witness life from our own perspective.

What Makes a Story Unique

Even though stories feature these two recurring components—the hero and the beginning, middle, and end structure—stories vary wildly. If they weren't different, we wouldn't read them, listen to them, or watch them.

This is the beauty of stories. Even though they all follow a hero through a journey, they're different because the people who tell them are different. Who we are and the elements we include in our stories make them unique.

The very first storytellers were hunters. They told stories about the animals they killed for sustenance and described the mystical world that the animals went to when they died. Animals gave life to early man, and man showed respect in return. The stories the hunters told reflected their relationship with the animal kingdom.

In *The Epic of Gilgamesh*, you can spot numerous references to the relationship between the hunter and the animal, and the mystical world of the unknown. The story is a reflection of the primitive hunters' world, and the reliance on the natural bounty that sustained them, as well as the magical realm that "explained" what they did not yet understand.

As these primal folk turned from hunting to planting, the stories they told to interpret the mysteries of life also changed. The cultivated seed replaced the animal as the center of life. It became the magical symbol of the endless cycle. Even though the plant died, it was not the end, but a new beginning, for through the seed the plant was born again. The cycle of agriculture formed the economic basis of the Babylonian, Hittite, Canaanite, and Egyptian civilizations. Babylonian stories revolved around the planting world with the god of sun and justice, Shamash, the god of weather and storms, Enlil, and the father of earth, Kishar. With agriculture as the key to survival, it makes sense that their stories and gods reflected this.

But what about us?

Most of us don't need to hunt for survival. These days the only hunting we do is at the grocery store for Ben and Jerry's Chunky

Monkey. The only farming we know is a lawn that we mow once a week. So what's unique to us and our environment today and in the last hundred years?

We've had momentous historical events, including two world wars, the Great Depression, and major outbreaks of contagions like the Spanish flu and smallpox. We have seen the invention of the computer, the Internet, robotics, and spaceships. These are all new to our environment and have inspired stories like *The Social Network, Blade Runner, Star Wars, Saving Private Ryan, The Grapes of Wrath,* and *Twelve Monkeys.*

The stories we create are also influenced by our own unique personal experiences. There are always nuggets of gold from your own life to draw upon—like the time that bully tried to attack you with a butter knife in your backyard or the fireworks that you felt when you experienced your first kiss. We hear, read, and see things in ways that are unique to us, every single day. Each mind processes information in a slightly different way. We have our own story fingerprint.

You might be inspired to create a story that reflects the hardships of a family member's childhood—like the true story of my mom's family, which was so poor they had to heat up bricks, wrap them up in towels, and put them under their bedsheets to keep them warm at night. Personal experiences have often inspired movie classics, including *Stand by Me, A Christmas Story,* and *Pride and Prejudice.*

We create stories about positive and negative things that are important in our lives. Yes, we still tell stories with a hero and a beginning, middle, and end, but they always have a new spin. As soon as we feel that every story under the sun has been told, time passes, our environment changes, and . . . BAM! A whole new set of "stuff" exists for us to respond to. Enter new story. Rinse and repeat.

Many of Pixar's films were inspired by the world around us and the changes we've seen in the last hundred years. From superhero fiction, to the invention of the automobile, and even today's issues of overpopulation and growing mounds of trash, the environment we live in has sparked Pixar's collective imagination. Without modern ideas, inventions, or problems, movies like *The Incredibles*, *Cars*, and *WALL-E* simply would not exist.

No matter if it's a story about a cocky, insecure hero named Gilgamesh or Woody, and his nemesis-turned-best-friend Enkidu or Buzz, who together are battling evil and trying to understand their own mortality, we must recognize that all stories have important similarities. To tell stories effectively, we must use these similarities to our advantage, while injecting our personal experiences and environmental influences into the mix. They then become *our* stories; personal to us, but new to the world, providing a fresh take on a familiar message or lesson. But in order to do this, you must have a great hero that your audience can connect with. Many studies have been done about leadership, and in the end, what makes for a good leader is often what makes for a good hero.

Heroes Are...

So what makes for a great hero in a story? Joseph Campbell, in his book *The Hero with a Thousand Faces*, defines a hero as "someone that has given his or her life to something bigger than oneself." Whether your main character is a devoted customer, someone endorsing your company, a CEO, or a fictional character in a film, you need to create an emotional bond between your hero and your audience. To do this your audience must care about your main character and believe in their cause. Endearing your audience to your character elevates them from an ordinary person, CEO, or fictional character into a hero.

When done well, heroes can drive sales, strengthen brands, and make personal connections with consumers. We see it happen all the time. When people connect with a hero in a story, they want to drive the same car they drive, wear the same shoes they wear, eat the same food they eat. Heroes also don't have to be people, they can be animals, objects, or animated characters. How many times do kids watch movies with an animated character or object and later want to buy everything connected to that character, like toys, cereal, or even shampoo? But how do you create a likable hero that can make an emotional bond with all ages, genders, and cultures?

A great way to create likability for a hero or leader is by sharing what they were like as kids, or better yet, starting off the story with your hero as a child. This builds empathy in your audience because we were all kids once and can relate. You can use backstory, flashback, or any number of devices to reveal a piece of your hero's childhood. For example, in the first ten minutes of the film *Moana*, we see Moana as a toddler. We watch as she protects a little baby turtle trying to cross the hot beach to reach the cool ocean water. Moana creates shade for the turtle with a palm branch and kicks away a pesky bird that tries to snatch him up. Even Darth Vader became likable in *The Phantom Menace* simply by being shown as a young kid who likes to build robots and podracers. By sharing stories of what your character was like as a child, based on your own experience or that of other kids, you will create genuine likability. To crank up the empathy dial to eleven, add that your hero is also an orphan. Storytellers like Walt Disney, Roald Dahl, J. K. Rowling, and Ernest Cline have all used this technique, setting up their heroes as orphans or soon to be orphans in *Bambi, James and the Giant Peach, Harry Potter and the Sorcerer's Stone,* and *Ready Player One.*

You can even create likability for a "jerk" of a character by giving them at least one redeeming quality, such as being funny, or by sharing a backstory that explains how they came to be such a jerk. Even the darkest villains can become likable if you introduce a character more evil than they are. Why do you think Darth Vader must answer to the Emperor? An audience often cares for a hero when it sees them in the role of the victim.

Heroes are also good leaders. They are decisive, driving the actions of the story. A good hero inspires others—including the audience—to act. As soon as the hero stops making decisions, good or bad, that drive the story forward, we lose interest.

Like heroes in a story, leaders can also inspire others to action by sharing similar passions and interests. Politicians often connect to their audience by cultivating and highlighting traits that we can all relate to, like Bill Clinton playing the saxophone or Barack Obama playing basketball. Ronald Reagan was a fan of jelly beans, and George Bush Sr. despised broccoli. In politics, it's referred to as the "howdy factor." Highlighting their individual traits helps leaders to seem more human and better connect with the public, if only to say, "Howdy, I'm just like you." So, shared interests and passions as simple as music, food, or sports teams or as large and complex as social or environmental causes can inspire characters to follow your hero.

Leaders should strive to be hopeful and optimistic. Your protagonists must believe that their journey is toward something that is positive and possible, or there will be no character arc or progression. Protagonists may be suspicious or mean or frustrated, but they take on the fight or the journey because some small part of them believes that success is possible. Protagonists live the lives that we want for ourselves by forging ahead even when the road is rough.

Leaders have core integrity. They value things like truthfulness and fair play. Your protagonists must be true to themselves or be on a journey to becoming true to themselves, or they will not be likable. One technique that screenwriters use to create likable heroes is setting up a "save the cat" moment at the very beginning of their story. "Saving the cat" is when you show a character performing an act of kindness for a lower status character. Remember how toddler Moana helps the little turtle in the beginning of *Moana*? It's an effective way to build instant empathy and make a protagonist not only trustworthy, but worth rooting for.

In the first minutes of *The Incredibles*, we see a very cocky Mr. Incredible defeating a villain and saving the day, but we actually don't like him until he helps an old lady get her cat out of a tree. This small act of kindness shows that Mr. Incredible is more than just an arrogant superhero; he becomes likable. The "save the cat" technique was also used at the beginning of *Aladdin*, when we see Aladdin, charming and full of himself, share his only piece of bread with some orphans.

A company or leader often uses this "save the cat" technique by demonstrating small acts of kindness, like donating time and money to environmental and social issues, which creates an authentic bond with their current customers and future customers.

Leaders are valiant in support of those around them. Likewise, good protagonists honor companions who help them get to their goal by rewarding them financially and with praise. They know that the journey is hard and are grateful for any help in defeating enemies and overcoming obstacles. In the world of business, these rewards can take the form of bonuses, stock options, or promotions.

Leaders can fail. We admire heroes not because they succeed all the time, but because they never give up. My favorite film hero as a kid was Indiana Jones from *Raiders of the Lost Ark*. I even managed to piece together an Indiana Jones outfit, fully equipped with leather whip, fedora hat, and a World War II leather jacket (from my Uncle Joel, a navigator on a B-17 during WWII). Years later, while at Pixar, I decided to analyze the script of *Raiders of the Lost Ark* and study my hero, and I was surprised to learn that Indiana Jones failed constantly. He lost prized objects time and again. He lost the golden idol. He lost his hat, he lost his whip, he lost his assistants, he lost the girl, he lost the ark, he lost control of more than a few vehicles, and he even briefly lost his mind. He was constantly losing. I discovered that my favorite film hero actually failed during 80 percent of the film. I was confused. Why did I, and millions of other fans, think of Indy in such a positive light? The movie documents his failures right along with his successes, creating empathy. This has been going on in storytelling for thousands of years. The most beloved heroes and leaders in fiction, nonfiction, entertainment, and business are the ones who are vulnerable. They struggle, they fail, they prevail. Steve Jobs had plenty of failures, notably the NeXT and Lisa computers. Michael Jordan missed 12,000 shots and is still considered one of the best basketball players of all time.

When leaders give up on their dreams and goals, the audience begins to dislike them. You must communicate to your audience that your hero will keep fighting for what he or she believes in, till the bitter end. As Walt Disney said, "The difference between winning and losing is most often not quitting."

Leaders are good communicators. Heroes often don't have a choice; it is written into their DNA. They say what they feel. They are authentic, especially in times of trouble. They cry out for help. They call the enemy out into the dusty street. We relate to them, because they respond like we hope to. A hero also communicates to the audience what they have learned by the end of the story. What the hero learns at the end of the story encompasses the heart and theme.

Discovery often leads the hero to an epiphany. In *UP*, the hero, Carl, has his epiphany during the "crisis" in act 3, when all is lost and he chooses to look through his deceased wife's book of memories. As he turns through the pages, he reflects on their wonderful life together. When he reaches the last page he discovers a handwritten note from his wife that reads: "Thanks for the adventure—now go have a new one! Love, Ellie." This is Carl's epiphany moment. He realizes that he has to let go of his wife in order to continue living. As a leader you must share epiphanies with your employees, peers, and clients. These moments can communicate how you learned to be a better team player, innovator, or communicator.

Leaders are decisive, and heroes should be as well. When the chips are down, they make the call. Do I go left? Right? Do I attack? Do I lay in wait? Heroes don't wait around, because they know that failure or death will swallow them up. They don't hesitate or waffle, even if it is a decision that doesn't always work out the way that they had hoped.

Along with needing a hero to drive the action, you will need other characters such as mentors, allies, and villains to create a great story. Without Obi-Wan Kenobi, Leia, Han Solo, Chewbacca, C-3PO, R2-D2, and a dark villain like Darth Vader, the story of Luke Skywalker would have been pretty bland. (See the next chapter on how to create a successful cast of characters.)

- We connect to the hero's journey because it is a mirror and metaphor of our own journey, or one that we would like to take.
- The primary character of a story (hero or protagonist) is not always "heroic" in a traditional sense, but rather the "main fighter" or one involved in a struggle.
- We create stories about things that are important in our lives; things that affect us in a positive or negative way. What often makes stories different and new are simply the people who tell them.
- You need to make your audience care about your main character: What were they like as a child? What interests might they share with the audience? How might they help a character who is below them? Revealing these traits can help endear your heroes to your audience.
- Perfect characters are forgotten. The ones with flaws who keep fighting find a place in our hearts.
- Leaders are hopeful, have core integrity, value truthfulness and fair play, say what they feel, cry out for help, and call the enemy out when no one else will. Leaders are decisive.

- CHAPTER 7 -

Cast of Characters

I get by with a little

help from my friends.

–THE BEATLES

t was the spring of my freshman year when my college dean shouted out my name throughout the CalArts animation department, announcing "Bart Simpson's on the phone, Luhn! He wants to hire you!" This was how the dean announced all job offers coming in for animation students. Sure enough, I was offered a job to work as an animator on the third season of *The Simpsons*. (You may remember a few details of this story, which I shared in the Introduction, but I promise I am going somewhere new with it.) I discovered that one of the directors of *The Simpsons* saw my animated short and was impressed. The next day I met with the show's HR team in downtown Hollywood and was asked to take a drawing test, which consisted of drawing the Simpson characters. I passed the test and began work that next week. Other than working at a few part-time jobs during high school, this would officially be my first "real" job.

When I arrived at work on my first day I was greeted by a bubbly secretary, who led me to a windowless, low-ceilinged room with eight animators stuffed behind drawing boards. The room was peppered with toys, musical instruments, and crumpled up animation paper scattered on the floor. It was definitely not up to fire code. The director of the show, a wiry pale guy with a boyish face named Mark Kirkland, popped in and happily introduced himself, handing me my work for the week. My job, like all the other animators at the studio, was to animate twenty-five shots a week! Yikes! A "shot," in film or TV, consists of all the action and acting that occurs between "cuts." In animation, a shot can consist of one to hundreds of drawings! I remember staying late every night that week, just barely finishing all my work.

Then after I delivered my twenty-five shots on Friday, Mark Kirkland sat me down and proceeded to redraw over each one of them. I was certain I was going to get fired, but I didn't. Instead, he patiently shared with me the fundamentals of animating for TV and composing a shot. Mark became my first mentor in the working world. For the next year, he would equip me with the knowledge and tools I needed to complete twenty-five successful shots every week. While Mark helped me, I also became friends with my animation team, and they gave me the confidence to do my job with words of encouragement and affirmation. They were my allies.

Some of them were old-timers, with animation experience on TV shows like *The Smurfs* and *Care Bears*. At first these animation vets were friendly, then they turned cynical and bitter, warning me that there is no future in TV animation. Fortunately, others on my animation team were playful, like Matt Nastuk, a multitalented guy with John Lennon spectacles and disheveled hair, always injecting humor into the workday, challenging the status quo, and reminding us not to take things too seriously. "C'mon guys, it's not brain surgery. We're just drawing cartoons," he would snicker. Some animators were newbies like me and became confidants I could share my insecurities and doubts with.

Then there was the assistant director, Kim, a chain-smoking brunette who dated famous athletes and made our lives miserable. And for whatever reason, she had a special hatred for me. After tearing up my work in front of everyone, she would attack me personally, going on about my skinny exterior or pimply face. Of course, as soon as Kim left the room, the other animators would draw hilarious caricatures of her being a tyrant. I could never have gotten through that first year on *The Simpsons*, or be where I am today, without those mentors and allies.

Everyone has stories that are populated with memorable supporting characters. The sage old-timer, the crazy abusive boss, the young kid dreaming of glory. Heroes—be they fictional or real—need a supporting cast that helps the hero grow and confront challenges. Sometimes these characters provide advice, encouragement, or even physical objects that empower the hero to overcome obstacles and acquire their goal. At other times, characters become obstacles, keeping the hero from reaching the goal.

Archetypes

Some character types appear again and again in literature, plays, and movies. Here are the most common archetypes:

The Herald: announces a need for change in the hero's life and/or world. Sometimes a herald is a character but can also come in other forms like a letter.

The Guardian: tests the hero before they embark on their journey. Also known as the threshold guardian.

The Mentor: equips the hero with information about the world and physical or symbolic tools to defeat the villain and reach the hero's goal.

Allies: help the hero overcome obstacles, defeat the villain, and obtain the goal.

The Trickster: injects humor into the story, challenging the status quo.

The Shapeshifter: at first appears to be the hero's ally, but later betrays the hero.

The Shadow: is the hero's main obstacle, creating external conflict and threat. Also known as the villain.

My *Simpsons* story included these classic characters:

The Herald: the dean at CalArts announcing my job offer
The Guardian: the *Simpsons* HR team and the *Simpsons* test
The Mentor: Mark Kirkland, my director
The Allies: my fellow animators
The Trickster: Matt Nastuk, my fellow animator
The Shapeshifter: the cynical animation veterans
The Shadow: Kim, my assistant director

People read, watch, and tell stories, not because they are enthralled with the outline or the story structure, but because they are invested in what will happen to the main character and other characters in the story. This is the true emotional juice of what drives a story. Without this juice, the audience will lose interest. A main character and set of characters are truly what define the actions throughout a story.

In no way am I suggesting that you need to include *all* of these characters in your story. However, these archetypes show up often enough that you should look for ways to include them in your personal and professional stories. Sometimes you will be cast as the hero, while other times you will be part of the supporting cast.

So, what role do we play in the business world as salespeople, marketers, managers, and techies in the stories that we tell to our clients, customers, and potential business partners?

Our focus on success—whether winning in the boardroom, winning with customers, or winning in the market—often leads us to naturally cast ourselves in the role of the hero. We want to save our customers from grass stains on their white jeans. We want to swoop in with a faster car. We want to rescue them from the difficulties of their daily life with our new and heroic product or idea.

Companies and marketers so often get locked into this kind of tunnel vision that they don't realize a simple shift in narrative that might well change the way customers perceive them and engage with their great ideas.

Business is about service. Good businesses exist to serve people well in the course of their lives, lifting them up to do their best and often boosting their livelihood. Instead of assuming that you are the hero, rescuing customers from a lesser existence, what if you cast your *customer* as the hero in your story? What if "saving the day" or "getting the treasure" wasn't about you landing their business, but about *them* achieving what they want out of life? In sharing their own stories, companies forget that their products are not the real heroes.

The customer is the hero. (One exception: when the story involves the company's founders.)

As I shared in chapter 1, "The Hook," heroes have goals they want to accomplish because they care passionately about something. The more a character cares about their goal, the more we care for the character. Luke Skywalker is out to save the princess and defeat Darth Vader. Dorothy is trying to find the wizard so she can get back to Kansas.

Your customers have goals too. They want to be healthier. They want to spend more time with their family. They want to make money, look good, drive a safer car. When you cast them as the hero, you put business in its proper place and respect the agency and authority of your audience.

You are not left out of the equation. There is always somebody who helps heroes at the outset, who propels them toward the goal. There is the mentor. Luke needs the help of Obi-Wan Kenobi. Harry Potter needs Dumbledore. Dorothy needs Glinda, the Good Witch of the North. The mentor provides the hero with a new way of thinking and sometimes an important tool to assist them in reaching their goal. Luke learns how to use the force and gets a light saber. Harry learns how to cast spells and gets the cloak of invisibility. Dorothy learns how to be brave and gets a pair of ruby red slippers. The tool gives power but also, more importantly, it gives the hero confidence to strive toward and reach their goal. Sometimes magical items don't even need to work properly. When Dumbo gets the black feather from his mentor Timothy, the circus mouse, it doesn't "really" make him fly, but it gives him the confidence to do it on his own.

As a company, you mentor your customers on their path to success, providing insights and tools. It could be insights on how a company could build a stronger brand or connect more effectively with customers. Or it could be a better pair of jogging shoes that helps them reach their goal of staying fit and healthy, or a car with better gas mileage that helps them save money.

Mentoring isn't the only job you do. Heroes also need the help of allies throughout their journey. For Luke it is Han Solo, Leia, Chewbacca, R2-D2, and C-3PO. For Harry it is Ron and Hermione. For Dorothy, it is the Tin Man, Lion, and Scarecrow. Likewise your customers need courageous loyal help to achieve their goals.

Allies help main characters figure out how to use the tools they are given. They pick heroes up when they fall. They boost their confidence. Customers, just like heroes, need to be nurtured from time to time. You shouldn't talk down to or "at" customers; you should walk alongside them to help them become the best version of themselves. Companies should make a point of finding ways to follow up and establish a relationship. Great companies don't merely figure out how to sell you something. They become your ally and your friend.

You can also use archetypal characters to share lessons and communicate messages within your companies. You can tell stories of how mentors and allies in your life have inspired you, along with threshold guardians that entrusted you with small projects that led to a promotion. There may have been tricksters who lightened the mood at work. Don't be afraid to include shapeshifters and villains in your stories. These negative characters push heroes out of their comfort zone, inspiring them to be better versions of themselves. Billy Crystal said it best, "Without Goliath, David is just a punk throwing rocks." Let's be honest—a story without a villain is boring. Villains and obstacles help us grow. They make the hero more heroic, and the work of the mentors and allies even more important.

When heroes have antagonists, it pushes them to be better. What obstacles does your audience face? Anything that stands in the way of a goal or has opposing values can be a villain. Villains don't have to be mustache-twirling creeps. In the movie *Inside Out*, there is no traditional villain. Joy wants life to be happy, and it is only sadness that keeps her from it. Classic villains include Voldemort, Darth Vader, and the Wicked Witch of the West. Villains can be a group of people, an institution, or a government. An opposing force doesn't even need a face. Many movies involve man against nature.

Villains create drama and make the story fun. Great brands include villains and obstacles all the time. In 1984, Steve Jobs fashioned the first TV commercial for the Macintosh computer. It involved a dystopian future not unlike the one in George Orwell's novel *1984*. We see the shaved heads of the masses, marching along, working in a gloomy factory, being harangued by a black-and-white face on a giant screen. A woman comes running down the aisle, carrying a giant sledgehammer. With an Olympic spin, she catapults it into the screen. It's as if all of the workers have been awakened from a nightmare. The punch line was the announcement of the Macintosh computer's debut and that "1984 won't be like *1984*." Without overtly saying it, Jobs cast IBM as the villain. Apple's new computer would bring individuality and personality to the age of computing.

Invoking Characters

So how can you develop characters for personal and professional stories? A technique that works for me is called "invocation." It's the process of invoking memories of people and characters that are locked away in your cobweb-covered memory. The first step of this exercise is to write down a list of favorite people in your life, such as teachers, relatives, and friends. Then write down a list of your least favorite people. Then for each person answer a series of four prompts invoking who they were:

It is . . . physically describe the person.
You are . . . identify the person's relationship to you when you met.
Thou art . . . tell us why that person is special to you.
I am . . . describe where that person is today.

If you described your favorite teacher, their invocation might look like this:

It is a middle-aged artist with a neatly trimmed beard, glasses, and colorful clothes.
You are my high school art teacher.
Thou art the one, outside of my family, who gave me the confidence that I could make a career as an artist.
I am retired from teaching at high school and happily painting in a rented art space in the San Francisco Bay Area.

Along with invoking characters that are people, you can invoke characters that are animals or inanimate objects. For example, you could invoke your favorite childhood toy or favorite pet. It really makes no difference, as long as the character or characters possess easily identifiable human traits that the audience can relate to. They can be toys, computers, cars, animals, as long as people can identify with them in the same way they would with humans.

Woody, an old pull-string cowboy toy, is not human but still has easily identifiable human traits that we can all connect to. He feels sadness, joy, and jealousy, as do we all. When creating a character, don't worry about what shape, size, or entity it is, as long as the audience can connect with them on an emotional level.

Great filmmakers, writers, artists, musicians, dancers, and other visionaries understand the power of finding that emotional juice in a character's story that can trigger an emotional response from the audience. There are many ways to do it, and many tools in the toolbox to choose from.

A skilled artist knows that he or she must connect on an emotional level with the viewer, and that all the beautiful draftsmanship, color, and composition won't amount to a hill of beans without a character who resonates with the audience.

Painter Norman Rockwell created a deep connection with viewers by finding ways to portray familiar and moving stories using characters' faces, postures, and settings. Stories of being in love, being afraid of going to the dentist, and arguing over a game of poker. People love his paintings because they connect with them on an emotional level. The same goes for the characters Michelangelo painted on the ceiling of the Sistine Chapel, or Rodin's sculpture of *The Thinker*, or even Charles Schulz's characters Snoopy and Charlie Brown. All of these visual storytellers succeeded at connecting with people through the characters they created.

In the same way, musicians use instrumentation, lyrics, rhythm, melody, and harmony to connect with listeners through the characters they sing about. From sad cowboy songs to the righteous rebellion of rock 'n' roll, music can span the entire spectrum of human emotion, causing us to break down and cry or get up and dance.

Successful visionaries, inventors, and business leaders have also mastered the ability to connect their products and ideas to people through character. Steve Jobs is a perfect example. He turned a computer full of wires and computer chips into a character with personality. When the Macintosh was turned on, the computer greeted the user by chiming and displaying "hello" onscreen. It was friendly and personal. Even the exterior of the Mac was designed to look like a face. Jobs turned an inanimate object into a tool with character and personality that drew people in and changed the way they thought about computers.

To do this, you must create a character with a well-defined personality, digging deeper to discover who your characters are and what makes them tick. I usually spend the first pass on my story trying to figure out my hero's character arc. Once I've locked down how my hero is going to change in the story, I develop the personalities for the rest of my cast of characters.

For example, on *Toy Story 3* we focused our first writing pass on figuring out Woody's character arc, while glossing over our villain, a pink stuffed toy named Lots-o'-Huggin' Bear. Then after our first pass, we explored why Lots-o'-Huggin' Bear was so cruel to the other toys at Sunnyside Daycare. This is when invoking past characters in your life comes in handy. As we brainstormed how and why Lotso became the way he was, the story team shared with one another our own childhood bullies. Usually bullies and villains have some type of backstory or inciting incident that made them become bad.

We also brainstormed about our favorite childhood toys, which led me to think about my son's favorite childhood toy, which was a stuffed plush rabbit with a blue vest and pink bow tie. My son loved his stuffed rabbit so much, that he carried it in his mouth by its two long ears wherever he would go. Until one day, when he was about five years old, we went on a vacation to Disneyland and when we got back home we couldn't find his stuffed rabbit. We searched the car, we called the hotel, I even called Disneyland, but no rabbit. So I searched toy stores, after first checking in with my dad of course, and eventually tracked down another stuffed rabbit toy at a store three hours away. I made the drive the next day, and thank goodness found the rabbit with an identical blue vest and pink bow tie. It was perfect, minus the wear and tear my son had put the original toy through. So I frayed up the new stuffed rabbit's ears with a pair of scissors and dragged his nose across the sidewalk to age him up a bit, and my son never knew the difference. But years later, I wondered what it would be like if the real stuffed rabbit resurfaced. This was part of the inspiration for Lotso's backstory in *Toy Story 3*.

We fashioned a backstory about how Lotso was once loved by a child, until one day he was accidentally lost on a road trip when his owner's family pulled over at a rest stop and the child spent some time playing with her toys. But when the family returned to the car to drive home, the child accidentally left her toys behind at the rest stop, including Lotso. Lotso searched for his owner, and after months finally found her, only to discover he had been replaced by an identical pink stuffed bear. Lotso was devastated. His heart broke and he snapped, changing from a lovable stuffed bear into a hateful character vowing never to love another kid again.

When exploring a character, analyze who your character is. Explore all sides. Here are a set of questions that can help you create more fleshed out and authentic characters.

Who Is the Character?

Passion: At the beginning of the story, what does your character *want* more than anything else in the world?

Fears: Often, underneath ambition and a strong positive emotional drive, a character harbors a fear of the opposite and negative result. What does your character fear in life?

Positive traits: What is your character good at? Traits like confidence, being funny, loyal, or passionate.

External traits: What set of attributes was your character born with or born into? Is the character naturally attractive? Charismatic? Wealthy?

Flaws: What weaknesses does the character have? Can the character be arrogant? Timid? Obsessive?

Dark side: What is the worst trait the character possesses, or the lowest low they are capable of? Would they lie? Steal? Kill to get what they want, or to avoid what they fear most in life?

Traits admired in others: What traits does the character *need* in order to be redeemed?

The emotional juice in a story all comes back to the fears and/or deeply rooted passions that drive a character throughout the story.

Let's use Woody in the *Toy Story* films as an example in our "Who Is the Character?" exercise.

Who Is Woody?
Passion: being Andy's favorite toy
Fears: being abandoned
Positive traits: leader, smart, compassionate

External traits: charismatic, has a pull cord, a collectible
Flaws: bossy, arrogant, worrier
Dark side: lie, maim, steal
Traits admired in others: confidence

Here is another example using Marlin, Nemo's dad, from *Finding Nemo*:

Who Is Marlin?
Passion: being a good father to Nemo
Fears: losing loved ones
Positive traits: loving dad, protective
External traits: unable to get shocked by a jellyfish
Flaws: pessimistic, overprotective
Dark side: resentful, hateful
Traits admired in others: optimism, being carefree

By analyzing a character in this way, you will have a much easier time knowing how to write dialogue for them and how they would react in different situations.

Now think of a bully in your life, or someone that picked on you in school. Mine was my next-door neighbor, Ernie. What a jerk. Think about why your bully or nemesis was a jerk. What made him or her tick? What might have been their passion? What about their greatest fear?

If you can't think of one, then maybe *you* were the bully. Shame on you! Either way, I'm sure you can think of someone who picked on you at some point in your life. Complete the exercise below using your bully.

Who Is Your Bully?
Passion:
Fears:
Positive traits:
External traits:
Flaws:
Dark side:
Traits admired in others:

This is a valuable exercise for developing a villain, hero, mentor, allies, or any other character for a story. Simply use people from your life as inspiration. For example, your childhood bully could inspire your story's shadow/villain, then take artistic liberties to adapt your bully to fit the story you want to tell.

Recently, my uncle Jeff shared with me a story about my dad's bully, Tommy Sparks. His story was not only entertaining but also communicated a theme about facing and overcoming your fears. Here's his story:

I was five going on six the first time I took a punch in the face.

It all began in 1958 when my older brother, Mark, due to a severe lisp, stuttering problem, and the physique of a toothpick, was getting relentlessly picked on by the school bully, Tommy Sparks. Tommy didn't have a full beard yet, but even at ten years old, he had wisps of facial hair that grew from his pimply red-blotched face along with a head full of scruffy black hair. But all of that was secondary to his oversized barrel-shaped body, pudgy arms, and menacing toothless grin. Tommy Sparks was a bully that pushed other kids around for fun, especially my older brother.

Tired of hearing about Tommy Sparks and afraid that his son would become a mousy wimp, my dad brought home the Jack Dempsey endorsed Everlast Boxing Kit. The kit included a heavy bag, a speed bag, two pairs of gloves, and an illustrated how-to book showing stances, jabs, uppercuts, and knockout blows. My dad set it all up in the garage and told Mark to train himself. He said, "The next time some kid starts to say something bad to you, drive your fist through his nose all the way to the back of his head. Don't even let him finish his sentence."

This came from my dad, who had earned pocket money in high school by fighting every Friday night at a "smoker" in Oakland, California. A "smoker" was a place where grown men would gather in a back room of a warehouse and pass around a whisky bottle while kids lined up taking turns fighting in a makeshift boxing ring. The back room was thick with cigar smoke and sweat as the grown men shouted and laughed while the boys walloped each other. In the best smokers, the winner got ten bucks and the losers got five. But you could get tips if you were really scrappy, and my dad did pretty well, even though his nose got busted a couple of times. Ten dollars was a lot of money in the 1940s. So for my dad, telling his ten-year-old kid to learn how to box wasn't an unreasonable request; it was an investment plan.

Every day after school, my brother Mark practiced punching the heavy bag, imagining it was Tommy Spark's face. What was missing though, was a living, breathing opponent. Although only six at the time. I had already displayed my fighting prowess by soundly defeating my inflatable "Bobo the Clown" on numerous occasions. In fact his red squeak nose was worn out by my fearsome right overhand punch. In short, my brother and I were totally clueless.

It happened in the garage. Mark put the gloves on me and told me to insult him. My arms were hanging loosely at my sides. I only got a few words out before he slammed me in the face. I stumbled back into the bicycles and went down. The punch was nothing, just a padded push that knocked me off balance. It was the bicycles that scratched me up. While I was scrambling to get to my feet, Mark rushed over to help me. He had already started crying. We both agreed not to tell my parents about it.

Just a day or two after Mark and I had retired from boxing, we encountered Tommy Sparks on the outskirts of our neighborhood. Tommy was standing on his tilted porch with a bucket of red paint in one hand and a dripping brush in the other. He was painting a splintered window frame. The kids in the neighborhood nicknamed Tommy's home "Hillbilly House" because it was so old and dilapidated. It faced an area we called "the Hills," where people discarded big things like washers and car parts, and developers dumped piles of debris. That was where Tommy and his mother lived.

As we sped by Hillbilly House, Tommy swung a fully loaded brush of paint at us. The flying red paint splattered all over my brother. It wasn't just a little drop or two, it was a series of globs. Big bloodred globs. Furious, Mark pedaled home. I followed.

Once we got back to our house, Mark wiped the paint off his face, hair, and bicycle, but it wouldn't come out of his flannel shirt or new jeans. This was a disaster because our dad was sure to get the truth out of us and it wouldn't go well. Mark had not used his fists to solve the problem. Tommy was scary, but our dad, when the vein started throbbing on his forehead, was worse. That's when Mark decided upon a suicide mission.

We looked for weapons and Mark happened upon the old folding knife in my dad's toolbox that we were forbidden to play with. It was dirty, not very sharp, and the blade didn't lock, so if you tried to stab something or somebody with it, you'd lose a finger or two. We had often imagined that my dad had carried it from island to island during World War II. This was probably not true. But it was, after all, a knife and better than brandishing a screwdriver or a hammer.

We got back on our bicycles and rode towards Hillbilly House. On the way my brother stopped and told me not to tell Tommy that he had a knife. Mark had learned from TV that surprise was the key to victory. Apparently Mark had a plan, but he didn't share it with me. We approached from the Hills and stood straddling our bikes outside Hillbilly House while Mark yelled at Tommy to come out. Mark turned to me and repeated, "Don't tell him I have Dad's knife."

Tommy and his mother came out and stood on the tilted porch. "What's wrong?" asked Mrs. Sparks. I should describe Mrs. Sparks in detail, but it would be repetition. Suffice it to say that there was a creepy family resemblance between Tommy and his mother, except she was bigger in every way.

Mark was trembling and he got into one of his stuttering loops while trying to describe being splattered with paint. Mrs. Sparks narrowed her gaze and put her hands onto the splintered railing. She leaned forward to see Mark's shirt and pants. "Come closer," she said. I'd seen enough traps on TV to know that certain death was imminent, so I shouted, "My brother has a knife!" Oddly, Mrs. Sparks didn't react, probably because both she and Tommy each carried one. But I'd just given away Mark's element of surprise. Mark did not move closer. "Tommy splattered me with paint!" he yelled. Actually it was a kind of squeak, not a yell.

With a look that meant business, she raised her voice and said, "Come here, let me see." Mark and I walked over and she looked at the red paint all over Mark's clothes and what remained on his face and hair.

"Tommy, did you do this?" she asked, while looking down at Mark.

"Yes," he said.

At that moment, without even looking at Tommy, she gave him the back of her hand so hard that he fell into a chair. It tilted backward and his head hit the wooden wall with a loud hollow sound. Tommy Sparks was trembling and starting to cry.

"Take off your clothes and I'll wash 'em," she said to Mark. There was no hesitation. Mark was petrified of Mrs. Sparks and peeled off his clothes as fast as he could. Stripping in front of Mrs. Sparks was not nearly as bad as having her rip off his clothes in public. Her voice was flat and emotionless and loaded with the power of a coiled spring. "Come back and get 'em tomorrow. Tommy! Get that can of thinner. RIGHT NOW, BOY!!" Then Mark and I rode home as fast we could. Mark was in his underwear, with my shirt wrapped around his waist all the way home.

The next day, we rode our bikes back to Hillbilly House but kept as far away as we could. On the chair, where Tommy had landed after being backhanded, we could see Mark's clothes washed and folded. Tattered curtains moved in the house. Someone was watching and waiting. "Let's go," said Mark as he jumped onto the pedals of his bike and rode over the hills and through the debris, straight at the house. He pedaled with a determination I'd never seen in him before. Other kids in the area stopped what they were doing and watched as my brother stepped off his bike while it was still rolling, as cocky boys did, and walked up the stairs to get his clothes.

The door of the house opened. Tommy Sparks came out. I saw Mark put his hand into his pocket to make sure the knife was there.

"I'm sorry. I didn't mean to splatter paint on you. It was an accident," said Tommy as he looked down at the weathered porch floorboards. "TOMMY!!!" came a thunderous yell from inside the house. Tommy shuddered.

Tommy Sparks raised his chin enough to stare at my brother. They looked right into each other's eyes. "Mark, I am very sorry I splattered paint on you. I should never have done that 'cause you weren't hurtin' me none. I had no cause." Tommy extended his hand to Mark.

My brother didn't flinch. He released his grip from the old knife and grasped Tommy's hand. "Do you wanna ride my bike?" Mark asked.

That's the day that two big things happened: Tommy and my brother became friends with a mutual fear, Mrs. Sparks, and Mark's stuttering and lisp went away. In a year the whole episode was forgotten.

In my uncle's story, my dad learned to face his fears, going from timid to brave, while my uncle learned that anyone, even his brother, could transform a bully into a friend. Remember, your customers, clients, and prospects are all heroes in the making, and you are in a unique position to identify their obstacles, come alongside them, and use a great story to give them the tools they need to succeed.

- People read, watch, and tell stories not because they are enthralled with the story structure, but because they are

invested in what will happen to the characters in the story. This is the emotional juice that fuels a story.

- For any hero (fictional or real) on a journey, a supporting cast can help the hero grow and be challenged. Characters in proximity to the hero can provide advice, encouragement, or even physical objects to empower the hero to overcome obstacles and acquire the goal. Characters can become obstacles as well, further challenging the hero in reaching their goal.

- Archetypal characters (heralds, guardians, mentors, allies, tricksters, shapeshifters, shadows, etc.) show up often enough that we should look for ways to include them in our personal and professional stories.
- As salespeople, marketers, managers, and techies, when we tell stories to our clients, customers, and potential business partners, we too often present ourselves as the hero, saving the customer from a lesser life.
- When your customers are cast as the hero, it takes the focus off of selling them on something and puts the focus on their needs and goals. Products are generally not the real hero, but they can help the hero achieve their goals. When you cast a person as the hero, you put business in its proper place and respect the agency and authority of your audience.
- What are your customers' goals? How are you an ally or mentor for reaching those goals? What obstacles do your customers face? How can you help them conquer those obstacles?

- **CHAPTER 8** -

Inspiring Creativity
in the Workplace

When people aren't having any fun,

they seldom produce good work.

—DAVID OGILVY

When I was hired at Pixar in my early twenties, there were only about eighty employees. Wanting to keep us away from the politics of Hollywood, Steve Jobs chose to rent out a commercial building in Point Richmond, a small city on the shores of the San Francisco Bay. It was in an area where ships had been built in World War II, but had since fallen on hard times. The large cement building seemed like an unlikely place for us to do something great, but the isolation and the cheap rent checked the boxes.

At this time Pixar was far from being a household name. We were just a company creating dazzling 3-D logos. Occasionally we would score a gig to animate a TV commercial for a company like Lifesavers or Listerine, but other than that we were relatively unknown. But we had an idea to do something great. We wanted to make the first CG feature animation film ever. Those first years working at Pixar were magical and would set up the Pixar culture for the next thirty-two years.

It was those first eighty employees who transformed the drab commercial building in Point Richmond, full of run-down grey cubes and dimly lit hallways, into a thriving workspace where *Toy Story*, *A Bug's Life*, *Toy Story 2*, and *Monsters Inc.* would be created. Steve Jobs and the other leaders at Pixar encouraged us to personalize our work environment. So we brought in old couches, Ping-Pong tables, video-game machines, and toys! We built tiki bars, cereal bars, and even a twelve-foot tree out of chicken wire, foam, and felt. In between animating shots on *Toy Story*, we constructed elaborate costumes for the Pixar Halloween party and held daily scooter races through the Tron-like maze of hallways in our building. We drew giant cartoons on the walls, filmed ourselves acting out hilarious irreverently funny puppet shows, and brought our pets to work. The studio wasn't just our workspace, it was our playspace, and because of this we enjoyed spending time at the studio, working and playing. The only thing that kept us from hanging out at work all the time was having to go home and wash our clothes or having to evacuate the premises because the oil refinery next door exploded again and everyone in the city was told to leave immediately so as not to get poisoned.

The Pixar culture didn't just magically appear, but was an outgrowth of several ingredients blended together. The first was CalArts. Many of us that went to CalArts were hired to work at Pixar, and we brought the energetic spirit and creative freedom of that environment, even if it came with a little dirt under the fingernails. That CalArts culture was then blended with the innovative culture that Steve Jobs brought from Apple.

Third, a passion for technology and film came from Industrial Light and Magic (George Lucas's special effects studio), where the idea for Pixar originated out of the computer graphics department in the early 1980s. This collision of creativity, innovation, and technology formed the Pixar culture.

Whether you work in entertainment or business or any other field, you want a workplace that inspires creativity and supports innovation—and teammates who understand, support, and motivate one another. While easier said than done, the good news is that it *can* be done! I believe that Pixar's track record for growth, success, and taking calculated risks (that have largely paid off) was made possible because Steve Jobs established a workspace that empowered us to perform on all creative cylinders. It's not like Pixar has a monopoly on creativity in the film industry. There are thousands of creative people working in Hollywood and elsewhere, but the reason Pixar has been so successful is because its employees were given the freedom to be their best. Remove this creative freedom and happiness, and success will plummet, even in a place like Pixar.

Inspiring creativity in the workplace comes down to three important things: transforming the physical environment, eliminating the fear of failure, and encouraging innovation.

Physical Environment

Physical environment matters. What you see, what you smell, what you hear, the walls, the lighting, the furnishings, the floor plan—all of these small details add up to form a workspace that is going to encourage or discourage creativity. Whether your organization's workspace serves eighty employees or eight thousand, there is always a way to improve on it.

After the success of our first couple of Pixar films, the company team grew and we needed a bigger space. So Steve located a plot of land across the bay from San Francisco that was once home to the Oakland Oaks minor league baseball team. The plot had fallen into disarray after the Dole canning factory moved in and leaked toxic waste into the ground. Always looking for a bargain, Steve purchased the land and broke ground on our new Pixar building.

After scraping and hauling away ten feet of polluted dirt, Steve designed the workplace we would all share, and his ideas sprung directly from what had failed at Apple. At Apple, people tended to scurry to their private corners and lock themselves behind office doors all day—not a good environment for promoting community, innovation, and happiness. Any team spirit that existed was not championed or nourished. Sometimes when you give people too much space and comfort, in spite of their best intentions, they choose to withdraw. Jobs didn't want to see that happen again.

As a result, the bathrooms and the cafeteria in the new space were designed to be in the center of the building. What that did was create a way for people to run into each other. When people left their offices during the workday, they would smile, say hello, and talk about what they were working on. They might even find a sympathetic ear or get help solving a problem. The floor plan encouraged spontaneous creative moments and the cross-pollination of ideas.

Setting up physical elements, like furniture and fixtures, in a work environment also matters. Start small. For example when a meeting is held at a rectangular table, either the person with the elevated status chooses the end position, or the person who sits at the end is given instant status above the others at the meeting. A pecking order is established, even if only subliminally, and the people at the meeting play into that hierarchy. In trial juries, researchers have found that whoever sits at the end of the table is more often than not elected jury foreman. Any environment where people are not focused on best ideas or solutions, but on pleasing the king or queen, or *being* the king or queen, undermines teamwork. To promote true teamwork, where people have equal say, use round tables to eliminate hierarchy.

At CalArts, creativity and community were cultivated by allowing students to make personal spaces their own. As a freshman at CalArts, I transformed my six-by-six-foot work cube into a tiki room adorned with all things I loved and would inspire me to create my first animated short. My fellow CalArts students did the same. We took this creative culture with us to Pixar, extending the same concept to our workspaces there. As a result people turned their offices into conversation starters that expressed their personality and kept them excited to come to work every day. Pixar employees created all manner of personal spaces, from jungle caves and speakeasies, to the inside of a crashed airplane and a Lego castle. Again, this served to foster conversation and creativity, and brought people together for a common purpose. People are most creative and innovative when they are surrounded by things that make them happy.

Eliminating the Fear of Failure

So many people operate day to day from a place of fear. Afraid to take chances, afraid to innovate, and afraid to be unique. But why? It all goes back to childhood. As kids we quickly discovered that when you do something out of the norm, like being inventive or creative, you risk getting picked on or bullied. We also are taught in school that if you don't answer the questions the "right" way you get an F. The message: if you try new things you risk getting ridiculed by your peers or failing in school.

Fortunately for me, I was encouraged to be a misfit by my dad. My dad and the rest of my family embraced and even encouraged me to be creative and different. This is why I wanted to go to CalArts like so many other creative people, because we heard it was a place where you were encouraged to create, fail, and build new things. This is the same reason why so many talented people in the world flock to companies like Google, Apple, and Pixar, because these companies take chances.

Unfortunately, this is not the case at many organizations. They have built cultures ruled by fear, where playing it safe replaces the impulse to take creative risks, and everyone is being too careful about what other employees or their bosses will think. These companies will never put a dent in the universe.

I'm not talking about the kind of fear that you feel when you're being pursued by a bear. That's panic-fear. I'm talking about the fear of appearing stupid, getting a reputation for being disagreeable, or worse—losing your job. Fear is not productive for you or the people you lead.

Just remember: if you empower your employees to take chances, they will fail. To be a truly creative company, you must take chances on ideas that might flop. This is part of the process. Learning from these failures could lead to even greater successes.

I have worked on numerous films and have generated thousands of ideas that never made it to the screen. But in many cases my ideas and drawings worked their way into the final films because they inspired others, linked up with previous ideas, or took a completely different view that made a difference. That's all part of the creative process.

Just as a company must test a new product a thousand times until they get it right, the same goes with new ideas and solutions. But fostering innovation means creating a culture in which all ideas are welcome, because it takes a few (or thousands) of bad ideas before you strike gold!

Most people believe that when you take chances you are just setting yourself up for failure. We often fear showing our vulnerable authentic side. We all want to save face. The dreaded performance review feeds our culture of fear. Faced with the risk of being laughed at or fired, we don't rock the boat. But failing is not a bad thing, and the great minds and artists of our generation not only welcome failure, they fail all the time! Great leaders all had to fail hundreds of times before they became better leaders. You must continually test and retest to make real progress.

One essential factor is creating a team that is open to other viewpoints, even if those viewpoints are contrary to your original plan. This requires patience and the belief that these different ideas, which may fail, will eventually culminate in a great idea.

Every film I have ever worked on always starts off as a mess. Even when I think I have learned from the mistakes I made on the last project, there are always new lessons I encounter. It's all part of the creative process. For example, in *Toy Story*, the character of Woody was originally an unlikable jerk. He treated the other toys like servants. Nobody who watched the early scenes liked him. The Disney Company decided they weren't going to fund the movie because Woody was so unlikable. This wasn't the reaction we were looking for! Our initial take was that we wanted Woody to become a nice guy by the end of the film, so he had start off in a bad place. Unfortunately, we went too far.

Luckily, we learned from our first attempt and fixed it.

Many companies are so afraid of failing, they put their energy into choosing one comfortable idea they are going to pursue, and they don't let go of it, even if it causes problems down the road.

When we first started developing *Monsters University*, the prequel to *Monsters Inc.*, we decided to star Sully, the big blue hairy monster, as the main character of the film. This seemed like a no-brainer being that Sully was the main character in *Monsters Inc.* So we began writing our film with Sully as the main character, but after months of writing and rewriting multiple versions with Sully as the lead, none of them felt right. In the end, we realized that this wasn't Sully's story but instead Mike Wazowski's, the adorable one-eyed green monster, with an inability to frighten anybody and a lifelong dream of becoming a "scarer" at Monsters Inc.

Up to that point we had put in a lot of effort, storyboarding and writing multiple versions focused on Sully. If we had made any one of those versions, the film would have been mediocre. But the Pixar culture saved the movie, allowing us to keep exploring until we reached the best version of our movie.

How would you feel if one of your employees or peers came to you partway through a project and pitched a completely new idea that was better? Would you have the courage and conviction to change direction? How often have you worked at a company that went ahead with ideas that you knew were mediocre, but you kept quiet because of fear?

The key is to fail early and fail fast.

In the space of one week, *Saturday Night Live*'s staff writes and performs an entire new episode, and always with a guest who brings their own unique style and history to the table. The first thing that the writers and actors do is to come up with the worst skits possible, and then perform them together as an icebreaker. The exercise leads to a lot of laughter, and a nonjudgmental environment in which creativity can grow.

Along with encouraging creativity in the workplace, I also encourage creative accountability in the workplace—a way to give and get useful feedback to nurture an environment where risks are welcome. Setting up a forum where you can give and get feedback is essential. A time and place where people can share their ideas during the early stages of development, and check in with other creative people to assure they are headed in the right direction, still reaching the target audience, and still communicating the feeling of the brand.

Knowing how to give good feedback is just as crucial as knowing how to take it. Good feedback requires the following:

- *Candor*—Be honest but be kind.
- *Mutual respect*—Remember that everyone is working toward the same goal, and is equally important in that process. Don't critique just to drop a bomb or feel better about yourself.

- *Timeliness*—Get back to colleagues quickly on their proposed ideas. If you wait too long to give your notes, they may have already gone in another direction, and now it's no longer possible to include your comments.
- *Brevity*—Don't write a novel of notes. Keep it clear and concise.
- *Limitations*—Always take into consideration the limitations of the project, like deadlines, cost, available tools, tech limitations.
- *A way forward*—Don't just evaluate the success or failure of their ideas, but suggest ways they could modify their ideas to make them better.
- *Ask questions*—Don't be afraid to ask questions. When you draw people out, it helps develop understanding and ideas. What is the takeaway they want? What do they want people to feel? Empower them to look deeper.

When seeking and getting feedback yourself, make sure you go to people who can truly speak to the specifics related to your project. People who have no experience screenwriting may not be the best choice for screenplay direction. There is a time for general feedback, and a time for specialists. Until you have worked things through with the specialists in your field, the "people on the street" might throw you off, either with too much praise or obscure demands not grounded in the needs of story.

Innovation

Everybody talks about innovation, but very few end up truly innovating. To innovate, you must be comfortable with failure time and time again. Innovating is most often easier for startups because they have nothing to lose, no money, no name, and no prestige. Startups are underdogs. They have a big advantage when they fight hard, and they can take the kind of risks that lead to innovation and success.

Unfortunately, for most people and companies, success is the kiss of death when it comes to innovation. The once innovative startup that makes it big becomes complacent, afraid to risk their status or track record. Leaders like Walt Disney, Steve Jobs, and Elon Musk are the exceptions. They continued to innovate even after becoming successful, because they were focused on more than just making money. They were focused on creating things that they believed the world would love, like a personalized computer, a theme park, or an electric car.

What is innovation, anyway? Innovation is creating something new that people will want even before they know what it is. It's about thinking outside the box and being revolutionary. Like automotive pioneer Henry Ford, who reportedly said, "If I had asked people what they wanted, they would have said faster horses." Innovation requires looking at the world from a different perspective, discovering unexpected obstacles, and solving them in unexpected ways.

For years, my dad took chances bringing new toys to the San Francisco Bay Area, like the Smurfs from Europe and "transforming" robot toys from Asia, before anyone asked for them. It was this innovative spirit that made Jeffrey's Toys special and surprising to its customers. Years later, Hasbro caught on, and saw the potential in these transforming toys and created their own version, "Transformers." But when you don't keep surprising people with something new, they start to lose interest and even turn against you. For example, one afternoon in the mid-1990s I was shopping in a grocery store in Hollywood, and while waiting in the checkout line, I overheard the conversation between the lady running the cash register and the guy buying his groceries. The grocery store clerk asked the shopper what he did for a living, and the guy said he was an animator at Disney. The grocery store clerk's first response was, "Please don't tell me you guys are making *another* animated musical?" It was painful to watch.

After working at Pixar for ten years, I could also see that we were starting to repeat ourselves by making mostly buddy movies, like Woody and Buzz in the *Toy Story* movies, Sully and Mike in *Monsters Inc.*, Marlin and Dory in *Finding Nemo*, and so on. Even though every film we had created so far was a blockbuster, we needed to shake things up and break the formula. So Pixar created *The Incredibles*. Why did we take the chance?

The public may say they want more of the same, but they don't always know what they want until you give it to them. Innovate before a grocery store clerk moans, "You guys aren't making *another* buddy film?"

Along with creating a brain trust at work for developing and perfecting ideas, there's a point when it's helpful to show your work to and get feedback from coworkers. Not just story specialists, but the next circle—tech people, HR, etc. Conduct surveys asking people if they can identify with the hero in your story, what the theme is, and whether anything felt strange. Then organize all the responses and the feedback to tighten up your story or change it.

At Pixar, six months before releasing a film, we would screen our films for non-Pixar audiences and look for anything we might have missed, like unclear story points or boring parts in the film that could be enhanced with humor.

Do everything you can to keep thinking like a startup. Creative companies that die are the ones who lose touch with risk-taking and the need to fight for survival. When things become predictable, it is time to remind yourself what innovation looks like, and open yourself up to taking chances once again. How many sequels are as good as the original film? Very few. People and companies consciously or subconsciously choose to play it safe, resting on their laurels. We see this happen all the time in entertainment and business.

Keeping Good Employees for a Long Time

It is worth mentioning that many companies struggle to find and retain talent. Above and beyond bonuses, or fatter salaries, people actually want to feel like they are learning and growing. Money might keep them close to home and stagnant, but challenge and new opportunities keep them fresh and growing.

Make a point to offer classes at work that are available to all employees, in an effort to keep them challenged. Sculpture classes, life drawing, culinary classes, improvisational acting, the list goes on. New learning experiences keep the brain fresh and excited. Along with offering classes at work, also empower your employees to start their own classes or events, like a photography class, yoga class, or annual car show.

Encourage original experiences outside of work. Offer education stipends to employees who take classes that inspire them to think outside the box, like writing classes, or who attend an event like Comic-Con or Burning Man. These adventures can even be wrapped into research and work trips, such as the two-week road trip a Pixar story team took on Route 66 in preparation for making *Cars*.

When you work for a company for a long time, you can develop an identity crisis. After ten to thirty years, you can't separate who you are outside of the company. This loss of identity can lead to a sense of despair. To battle this, find ways for yourself and others to continue having a life outside of work. For example, while working at Pixar, I continued to write and work on my own personal projects. I created a number of how-to-draw books for kids along with teaching story seminars for adults.

Some of my Pixar peers also had projects outside of work, like making short films and writing children's books. By allowing your employees to use their creative talents outside the company you will keep them happy and in return, they will bring that positive experience back to the office. Many top companies do this. Even if it creates competition for them in the marketplace, a good employee losing touch with their identity and passion is a far worse trade-off.

- Inspiring creativity in the workplace comes down to three important things: enhancing the physical environment, eliminating the fear of failure, and encouraging innovation.
- Increase the number of people sharing ideas by changing the furniture, the seating arrangements, or the order in which people participate.
- Design your physical work environment so people bump into one another, inspiring a cross-pollination of ideas to occur.
- We all fear it, but failing is not a bad thing. The great artists and companies not only welcome failure, they fail all the time themselves. To truly innovate, you must be comfortable with failure time and time again.
- Giving good feedback is crucial. It requires candor, mutual respect, timeliness, brevity, and a way forward.
- People want to feel they are learning and growing. What experiences and education are you offering outside of work?

- CHAPTER 9 -

Writing Tips and Techniques

You can't wait for inspiration.

You have to go after it with a club.

—JACK LONDON

Before our first daughter was born, my wife and I read tons of books on how to be great parents. Although we knew that everyone is a perfect parent until they have kids, we were determined to try.

We read books on the best ways to get your baby to sleep, eat, learn, plus other fun tidbits of baby trivia. For example, did you know that babies have super sensitive hearing when they're inside the womb and can recognize your voice when they're born? Or that when babies are born, they already know how to swim? Yep, swimming is built in their DNA. Sure, they're not going to bust out of the womb, swim a lap, and win a gold medal or anything, but they do know how to hold their breath, paddle, and float. So if that's the case, how come so many people don't know how to swim when they get older? Well, it might seem silly, but . . . they forget.

Just like a baby is born knowing how to swim, we're also born knowing how to tell stories. It's a natural instinct that's been a part of the human race for thousands of years. But just like forgetting how to swim, we can also forget how to tell stories. Nevertheless, with some simple guidance, clear instruction, and a bit of practice, we can all relearn how to be great storytellers—just like we can relearn how to swim.

I believe with the right tools, instruction, and practice anyone can become a better storyteller and writer. Here are a few writing tips as you embark on your journey as a storyteller, writing a screenplay, a book, a blog post, or delivering a pitch.

Write every day.

Write short, write mad, write poorly—just write. Clear your schedule for tomorrow and make writing a bigger priority.

Read.

Good writers are good readers. Read for variety. Find stories that move you. Twenty minutes before you sit down to write, read an author whose writing you wish was your own.

Schedule your writing time.

Write when you feel fresh and energized. Some people write early, some write late, some write after exercising. What are your distractions? Identify them and put them in your mental waiting room.

The first ten minutes is the hardest part of writing.

Work in short bursts of ten to thirty minutes. Don't linger, staring at the screen or pad of paper. Write the hardest or most enjoyable thing first, and just get something down. It is easier to work with something than nothing. Return later to revise, refine, and find new inspiration.

Are you a Planner or a Panther?

Planners plot out the story. They need to know where it is going before they write a single word. They tend to think about story more analytically. They need a skeleton to move forward, believing that their writing will benefit from having a plan. Panthers prefer to sit down without a plan and go go go, believing that the story will reveal itself and all the places it needs to take the reader by way of the writing process. The panther is more free-flowing, improvisational. Both planners and panthers write good stories. But it helps to know your tendencies and great to develop traits of both planners and panthers.

Panther Exercise

Set a timer for eleven minutes and write as fast as you can. Free associate. Don't worry about spelling or punctuation or making sense. Make strange word pairings. Put adjectives and nouns together that don't belong. Make silly sentences. Invent words. Write one expression over and over, changing one word each time. Type a name. Give the person behind the name a strange quirk. Push them through a doorway they have never crossed. Time is up. How many words did you write in eleven minutes? Next time try to write even more.

Planner Exercise

Find an otherwise boring story in the newspaper. Develop it into a story spine as if you have been hired by a major studio to turn it into a blockbuster movie. Like Alfred Hitchcock said, "What is drama but life with the dull bits cut out."

Quick In, Quick Out

Remember, people have a very short attention span. Whether you are writing a pitch, telling a story, or drafting a novel, get to the action as quick as possible. Once you are there, try to think how quickly you can get to the end of your story.

Emotion

Build to emotional moments. Use everything to tap into the emotions of your readers. Create belief but never demand it. Invite them into the story with good writing, but don't push them through the door with too many adjectives and adverbs.

"Use descriptive language and intonation to evoke emotion in storytelling."

—Jean Shepherd, *A Christmas Story*

Words Matter

- Active voice instead of passive voice keeps readers on the edge of their seats. PASSIVE: Burglaries were on the rise. ACTIVE: A man in a mask punches out a back window.
- Short sentence, long sentence, short sentence: let your writing breathe. Mix it up. Be aware of cadence.
- Paragraphs that are too long exhaust the reader. Too many short paragraphs are a distraction.
- A good scene is always building toward something, and every word matters.
- Big or fancy words are like pouring perfume on a flower.
- Adjectives and adverbs should be used sparingly.
- Don't tell readers what to feel—seduce them with your words. Let your story summon their feelings.
- Cut your work in half and see if it doesn't improve. We all tend to write too much. Ernest Hemingway strived to write short sentences, short first paragraphs, and vigorous English.

Editing and Rewriting

"By the time I am nearing the end of a story, the first part will have been reread and altered and corrected at least 150 times. I am suspicious of both facility and speed. Good writing is essentially rewriting. I am positive of this."

—Roald Dahl

How to Edit

- Edit for story: Improve the flow.
- Brevity: Trim your prose.
- Clarity: Write simply and clearly.
- Voice: Is it consistent? Believable? Inviting?
- Words: Smaller, more direct is better.
- Clichés: Use very rarely.
- Tenses: Make sure they are consistent.
- Adverbs: You can do with less.
- Adjectives: The more you use, the more they dilute the power of your story.
- Structure: Does every scene build to the next one? Do they all build to the finale?

I know that diving into writing and storytelling can be difficult, intimidating, and even scary. First drafts are always awful. Rehearsing your sales pitch in the mirror is awkward. But it does get easier. Trust me. We can all relearn how to be great storytellers.

Just keep swimming.

– EPILOGUE –

Now it's your turn! Have fun infusing storytelling into your personal and professional life, creating and telling stories that will be memorable, impactful, and transformative. Remember, the most powerful person in the world will always be the storyteller, whether you work at Pixar, a Fortune Global 500 company, or even a small family toy store.

– ACKNOWLEDGMENTS –

Like a hero on a journey, I relied on many allies, mentors, and specialists to help me reach my goal of writing an informative, accurate, and hopefully inspiring book on the art of storytelling for business. This cast of characters included my editor and ally David Drury, my mentors Jeffrey Luhn and Robert Luhn, my agents Ken Sterling and Barrett Cordero, my proofreader Katherine Rawson, my initial writing pal, Lisa Axiotis, and my talented wife, Valerie LaPointe Luhn. I'm also thankful to the team at Morgan James for heralding me into this adventure by encouraging me to write *The Best Story Wins*.

I want to also extend a tremendous thank-you to all my story allies and mentors throughout the years at *The Simpsons*, ILM, Pixar, and beyond. I have learned so much from all of you. I am eternally grateful.

And finally, a special thanks to my dad, grandpa Mannie, and other family members for allowing me to share their stories and love for business.

– ABOUT THE AUTHOR –

Matthew Luhn is a writer, story branding consultant, and keynote speaker with over 25 years of experience creating stories and characters at Pixar Animation Studios and beyond. Matthew's story credits include *Toy Story, Toy Story 2, Toy Story 3, Monsters Inc., Monsters University, Finding Nemo, UP, Cars, Ratatouille,* and other films and TV shows currently in development. Alongside his story work in Hollywood, Matthew also trains CEOs, marketing teams, directors, and other professionals on how to craft and tell stories for Fortune 500 companies, Academy Award winning movies, and corporate brands grossing billions of dollars worldwide. Matthew attended the world-renowned Character Animation department at Cal Arts in Los Angeles, and holds a BFA in Illustration from the Academy of Art University in San Francisco. He currently resides in Oakland, California.

To book Matthew for a story seminar, workshop or keynote, please contact: info@bigspeak.com or matthew@matthewluhn.com

CPSIA information can be obtained
at www.ICGtesting.com
Printed in the USA
BVHW07s1954190818
524547BV00003B/12/P